.be our guest

KATHLEEN BILLEN
KRISTIN VAN DE VOORDE-HEIDBÜCHEL

be our guest

THE AMBASSADORS OF BELGIAN HOSPITALITY

LANNOO

CONTENT

Foreword 7

Etiquette
– the rules of hospitality 9

7 cocktails and 3 appetizers
– pre-dinner, the Belgian way 19

Jan Vandenplas 20
Elderflower Kir 23
A Monastic Gin & Tonic 24
Nosy Nose 25
Rocking Raspberry 26
Belgian Mojito 27
Belgian Horse's Neck 28
Sweet Diamond 29

Dimitry Lysens and Aagje Moens 30
Nasturtium with shrimp milk 31
Mini Peking duck skewers 32
Red and yellow devils 33

■ Belgian wine, an ambassador in the making 36

7 top chefs create a menu
for 21 embassies of Belgium 41

Maxime Collard 42
Starter: Goose liver Maxime's way – Budapest 44
Main dish: Kudu of the Ardennes forests – Pretoria 48
Dessert: Lamington chocolate delight – Canberra 52

Gert De Mangeleer 56
Starter: Dim sum stars – Beijing 58
Main dish: North Sea sushi – Tokyo 62
Dessert: From Flanders fields – London 66

Bart De Pooter 70
Starter: Bacon and cabbage flamenco – Madrid 72
Main dish: When West meets East – Istanbul 76
Dessert: A sweet dessert from the medina – Tunis 80

Sang Hoon Degeimbre 84
Starter: A Brussels waffle in Paris – Paris 86
Main dish: Wadi rum – Amman 90
Dessert: Millefeuille Namaste – New Delhi 94

Yves Mattagne 98
Starter: Berliner Art – Berlin 100
Main dish: The Emir's 'Coucou de Malines' – Abu Dhabi 104
Dessert: Chocolate waltz – Vienna 108

Pierre Résimont 112
Starter: River trout for Rio – Rio de Janeiro 114
Main dish: All ... deer ... lead to Rome – Rome 118
Dessert: The strawberries of Wépion meet Thailand – Bangkok 122

Lionel and Laurence Rigolet 126
Starter: Filet Américain 'Comme chez nous' – Washington 128
Main dish: Veal shanks 'Art Nouveau' – Moscow 132
Dessert: Pancakes for 'Orange-Nassau' – The Hague 136

■ Beer, the ambassador of Belgian diversity 140
Belgian beer for dummies 141
Daniella Provost 143
Beer on your buffet table 145

7 simple dishes for a walking dinner 147

Albert Verdeyen 148
Basic preparation for all kinds of 'stoemp' 150
Cod fillet with pickles sauce 150
Asparagus puffs 151
Coucou de Malines with Ardennes ham 152
Endive croquettes 153
Mussels croquettes 154
Royal stoemp with lobster and fine herbs from the garden 155
Flemish beef stew with fries and mayonnaise 156

■ Belgian fries, an ambassador of Belgian unity 160

7 healthy recipes for a business lunch 163

Arabelle Meirlaen 164
A pair of drinks 'Mens sana in corpore sano' 166
Spring rolls 167
Tomato mosaic 168
'Ayurvedic' lobster from the Belgian coast 169
Back to the roots 170
Vegan cheese platter 171
Fragrance of 3 fruits 172

Geert Van Hecke 176
Bouchée à la Reine of the 21st century 178

■ A special ambassador: Her Majesty Queen Mathilde 180

7 cosmopolitan dishes to share 183

■ Diamonds, a sparkling ambassador for Belgium 184

Seppe Nobels 186
Starter: Starter of the purest carat – Copenhagen 188
Main dish: 'Mazel und Brucha' – Tel Aviv 192
Dessert: Antwerp 'pain perdu' Canadian style – Ottawa 196

7 desserts sweet and salty 201

Paul Wittamer 202
Royal chocolate cake 204
Tricolour fruit jelly 206
The 'Misérable' 207
A feast of mini tartlets 208

■ Chocolate, Belgium's most excellent ambassador 210

David Maenhout 212
Chocolate lollipops 214
Cold minty chocolate drink 215
Belgian brownie with nuts and candied fruit 216

Nathalie Vanhaver 218
Belgian cheese platter 220

Belgian hospitality on the web 222
Thank you to 223

FOREWORD BY KATHLEEN BILLEN & KRISTIN VAN DE VOORDE-HEIDBÜCHEL

Kathleen Billen has had a career as an attorney specialising in tax law. Together with her husband Ambassador Johan Verkammen and their four sons, she has travelled around the wide diplomatic world. From Hong Kong over Brussels to Lebanon, Senegal and most recently Canada. During her stay in Dakar, she wrote a travel guide about Senegal with the best Belgian addresses.

Dr. Kristin van de Voorde-Heidbüchel is a dentist and specialist in orthodontics. She is married to Baron Willem van de Voorde, Honorary Secretary to the Queen and Ambassador of Belgium to Vienna, and more recently to Berlin. With her husband and their children Alexander, Bruno, Elinor and Sibylla, she discovered Germany, Japan, Austria, Slovakia and Slovenia.

Hospitality is a very important concept in every language and in every culture. New encounters, generosity, respect, conviviality, gastronomy, etiquette, these are just a few facets of a hospitable experience. Gourmet Belgium, with its rich gastronomic heritage, is without a doubt a welcoming country at the heart of Europe.

All over the world, Belgian diplomats and their partners have the privilege to meet and receive personalities from the most diverse backgrounds. They thus contribute to promoting Belgian hospitality and gastronomy abroad. As Belgium has so much to offer in this field, the men and women who represent our country do this with great pride, to further enhance the country's image abroad. Didn't an American president once say, *'It is easy to love a country famous for chocolate and beer'*? Indeed, in the diplomatic as well as in the business world, people who have already got to know one another around a gourmet and welcoming table in a friendly atmosphere, will exchange their views more smoothly, have more pleasant negotiations and iron out obstacles more easily.

And what an amazing table it can be! It was impressive to have a chance to meet so many talented Belgians and to bring them together for this book. In their domain, each of them is an ambassador for our country, our culture and, also, our hospitality. You cannot deny that taking a break in our busy lives to enjoy each other's company around a friendly table, nourishes relationships and friendships ... and even love. Although it might be a passion and a talent to cook, mix cocktails, produce wine, brew beer, create new chocolate flavours, discover authentic cheese, design tableware, or make inspiring speeches, it has no real value if you cannot share it with others.

The greatest pleasure for us is to share this with you. In so doing, we unveil a little of what Belgium has to offer and how the embassies of Belgium, to the best of their abilities, try to put our country on the map by showing its hospitality. A very special thank you goes to the Federal Public Service Foreign Affairs, Foreign Trade and Development Cooperation who has supported our project from the start and to all our colleagues in the 27 Belgian Embassies and Consulates General of Belgium who kindly agreed to be involved.

.Be our guest!

Kathleen Billen   Kristin van de Voorde-Heidbüchel

.be our guest

Etiquette

THE RULES OF HOSPITALITY

THE RULES OF HOSPITALITY

Is there anything more enjoyable than having a good time in the company of friendly people? And who doesn't appreciate those little gestures that leave you feeling liked and appreciated? For centuries, rules of savoir-vivre and politeness have helped us humans to get along, and over the years etiquette has evolved, shaped by the culture, religion, ethics, social progress or, even, the personal sensibilities of the day. In other words, etiquette is constantly in motion.

It all started in prehistoric times when fire and knife provided the initial incentives for good manners; whoever held the knife cut the meat and distributed the pieces, thus creating a social hierarchy within the group. Respecting authority, maintaining harmony and observing certain rules were essential for survival. These basic precepts have never fundamentally changed; at most they have been fine-tuned to suit each new civilisation. The first traces of a written code of conduct date back more than two millennia BC to Ptahhotep, an ancient Egyptian philosopher. He stated that polite dealing with people is one of the founding virtues for a just and peaceful Egypt. In the crowded palaces of the Pharaohs, good table manners and the art of civilized conversation were strongly developed and highly prized, whilst in Asia Confucius regarded etiquette as key to maintaining harmony between the different layers of society. His teachings continue to be at the heart of many rituals in Asian business and family life where the principal aim is to show respect.

Also in ancient Greece and at the peak of the Roman Empire, an elaborate dining culture was established. Owning beautiful tableware and knowing how to behave at table became status symbols. For example, a smart Roman would always be in possession of his own table napkin. A lot can be learned about the time's etiquette from the interesting story 'Trimalchio's Dinner'. Petronius makes fun of Trimalchio's nouveau-riche character, describing how he comports himself as he tries to imitate the nobility with increasing ostentation. However, after one drink too many, Trimalchio's lowly origins surface, as he burps, breaks wind and tells tasteless jokes …

After the fall of the Roman Empire, monastic orders, rare beacons of refinement in this dark period, organised society in a much more austere manner. Etiquette as we know it today didn't spread across Europe until the return of the crusaders. At this time Arab culture was already very sophisticated, and it was a complete revelation to these knights in armour who only washed once a year at Easter. Delicious food, musical entertainment as they ate, rosewater to wash their hands, daily baths, perfumed oils, refined table manners and civilised conversation strongly contrasted with the harsh life in their home castles. Influenced by their oriental experience, a courtly culture developed, which the knights practised around their table, while out hunting and, also, in the pursuit of love. In courts (from where we get the term courteous) throughout Europe refinement was cultivated. In the court of Philip the Good visitors received a card outlining the rules of the court. This card was commonly known as the 'etiquette', or label, and the concept travelled to Vienna on the marriage of Mary of Burgundy to Maximilian of Austria and from there to the Spanish court. The Italian count and diplomat, Baldassare Castiglione, penned a particularly interesting guide entitled 'The Courtesan's Book' which became the bible of good manners during the Renaissance, and which set the scene for the 'British gentleman'. But that all pales in the face of the grandeur of Louis XIV. His royal courtiers, perfectly trained, and the sumptuous parties at the Palace of Versailles were replicated as far as St Petersburg. Table manners, conversations, uniforms – everything was prescribed and woe betide anyone who broke the rules. The light of the Sun King continued to shine for centuries and influenced the manners and social graces of the rich bourgeoisie who liked to impress with their cutlery, their glassware and their fine tableware. Until finally, during the reign of Queen Victoria in England, strict Victorian morality and manners took root and spread across the British Empire.

Until the Second World War, etiquette was intended to remind us of our standing in the social hierarchy, an idea that was about to change dramatically. Society was becoming more democratic, and equality between men and women was being promoted; this, along with an emerging globalisation, propelled etiquette towards a combination of courtesy, common sense and, above all, respect for others, regardless of class or rank.

So, whether you like it or not, etiquette endures. Also today, its role in human interaction cannot be underestimated, just as much in the home as in the most refined diplomatic circles. Thanks to a commonly understood code of conduct, it encourages respectful engagement with others. Etiquette also helps to promote a person's character. It can reinforce good points and help achieve objectives: think of a first date, a job interview or an important business dinner. The first impression – said to last only 5-7 seconds – often determines how someone will be perceived. No matter how much one tries to correct it subsequently, those first moments will define a person for a long time to come.

Below are a few of our favourite suggestions as to how to welcome guests, guided by the rules of etiquette. It is not meant as an exhaustive list of petty rules to observe. We prefer to outline a few guidelines to help you put your guests at ease, whilst allowing you to be as creative and flexible as circumstances dictate.

THE 10 COMMANDMENTS OF ETIQUETTE

Whether you are dining with a Minister or having Christmas dinner with your family, the following tips will always be useful

1. No matter what happens, **always put your guests at ease**. Start the evening abiding by the rules but be prepared to let a more informal ambience slip in. Your guests should, above all, be relaxed and feel welcome. Kindness and a genuine interest in those you have invited are important. And, of course, you would never pass comment on any possible mistake your guest might make. The well-known anecdote about Queen Victoria and the finger-bowl perfectly illustrates this. During a State dinner, a visiting African leader unwittingly drank from his finger bowl, and the Queen, in a gesture of impeccable courtesy, lifted her bowl and did the same. At the end of the day, etiquette is not so much a question of doing, but rather of being.

2. You may receive a **gift** from your guests to thank you for your invitation. The most common error, although always well-meant, is to say 'You shouldn't have' or 'There was no need'. Such a reaction negates the good intentions of the gift-giver. Instead, warmly thank your guest and unwrap the gift in front of them, especially if you sense that they may like to explain their choice or would simply appreciate seeing you are pleased with their present. You may like to share a gift of chocolates or biscuits with all your guests when serving coffee. If you receive flowers, put them in a place where they can be seen and admired. And of course a short thank you (even by text or email) the following day will always be appreciated and only takes a moment of your time.

3. Guests who arrive late or who arrive too early are very annoying and risk ruining your **timing**. However, 'too late' or 'too early' don't exist in the vocabulary of good hosts. Guests are always on time and always welcome; that's the message to give when they arrive a little stressed or embarrassed. A few nibbles and a drink will put them at ease and create a relaxed atmosphere while waiting for the other guests to arrive. Introduce each new arrival to those already present. Does this mean that all the guests should jump from their chairs with each new arrival? Men certainly should, if they can. While in principle women can stay seated, more often they also get up to greet the newcomers. If all goes to plan, then the guests should be ready to move to the table after about half an hour of chitchat. It is up to you to announce this, starting with your guest(s) of honour.

4. The aim of every gathering is to establish an engaging rapport among those invited. The host and hostess play an important role. When **introducing your guests**, don't confine yourself to names; try to say a few words about their areas of interest or expertise. In this way you will have already set in motion an interesting and rewarding conversation. But who should be introduced to whom? The rule of thumb is that the less important person is introduced to the more important. So broadly speaking, younger is introduced to older, junior to senior, less known to more well-known, etc. Depending on circumstances and sensitivities, you can certainly give free rein to your own interpretation and instincts. If you prefer not to make such distinctions you can always say 'May I introduce you to each other?' This way you are putting both people on an equal footing.

5. Etiquette is no longer constructed around **male and female** stereotypes. Courtesy extends to everyone, and if there are distinctions they tend to be based on importance and role rather than gender. Of course, it is customary and appreciated for a man to help a woman take her place at the table, especially at formal dinners. Just as it is polite to hold open the door for her or to let her go first. However, be careful, gentlemen – never let a lady go before you up the stairs. That way you will never embarrass her if she is wearing a dress or a skirt.

6. The **smartphone** is today's indicator of how aware of etiquette a person might be! Do you know the main reason a woman might be disenchanted after a date? It's that he can't keep his eyes off his phone and, even worse, is

texting during conversations. Such behaviour is a clear indication that the thoughts of the person sitting opposite you are elsewhere, and seemingly your company doesn't merit his full attention. Therefore leave your smartphone in your pocket or in your bag during dinner, preferably on silent mode rather than vibrate mode which can also disturb. If circumstances insist that you answer a message or an important call, it is polite to signal this in advance and to excuse yourself at the time.

7. Don't begin **to eat or drink** before everyone is seated and served and the hostess, or host, has started to eat or has asked everyone to start eating. Even though it might seem friendly and natural, the rules of etiquette do not permit you to say 'bon appétit' on formal occasions. It is the hostess, or the host in the absence of a hostess, who gives the signal to start eating by simply starting to eat and thus leading by example when it comes to which cutlery to use. They will also help themselves to more food as a signal for their guests to do the same.

8. Table manners are essentially a means of showing respect for others. They can take several forms. You are served something you don't like? Try to take a mouthful, or at least cut it up before leaving it on your plate; don't attract attention by explaining why you are not eating. Never season your food before you have tasted it. So that you don't bother your neighbour, try to keep your elbows by your sides. Elbows should only ever rest on the table between courses, and only when the plates have been removed. Wrists should lightly rest on the table or a little above it, never underneath as it suggests you have something to hide. Your feet should not bother any of the other guests. Therefore, don't stretch them too far in front or to the side. For your own comfort, don't bend them back too far beneath your chair, because that will cause your table napkin to slip to the floor rather than resting on your knees. Having to pick it up risks disturbing your neighbours. Butter your bread by putting a small piece of butter on your side plate, then break off a small piece of bread, no bigger than a mouthful, and butter it. Never butter a whole piece of bread and certainly don't open it like a sandwich. If there isn't a knife on the butter plate, use your own butter knife, which you should find on your side plate. If guests are serving themselves in turn, pass the serving dishes to the right, so that everyone can serve themselves from the left. Serve drinks to those sitting beside you before filling your own glass. If you must go to the bathroom, excuse yourself without offering any further explanation, or at most just say you are going to wash your hands. Try to keep up with the general pace of the table, so that you don't keep everyone waiting by being the last one to finish.

9. Finished eating? You can indicate this by placing your cutlery at the 'four o'clock' position. If you are only taking a break or the time to finish a conversation, or waiting to have another helping, then cross your knife and fork on the plate or put them on the right and left edges of the plate (the fork with its tines facing down). When you are finally leaving the table, put the table napkin, lightly folded, on the left side of your plate. Do not fold it carefully, as this gives the impression that you intend to return for another meal. And where should we have our coffee? According to classic etiquette, coffee is never served at the dining table. Winston Churchill was a persistent opponent of this rule because it interrupted discussions around the table. So let this depend on the ambiance and your reception area. After a formal dinner with many guests, a chance to regroup can be a welcome change.

10. Accompany your guest to the door, help them with their coat and wish them a safe journey home; these are the little touches that finish the evening in style. This is also the moment to exchange a few words that you might not have managed earlier in the evening. If a couple is hosting, then one should remain with the other guests; if you are on your own, then try to return to the remaining guests as soon as possible. The next day when your guest calls to say thank you, be very appreciative of their thoughtfulness.

7 SUGGESTIONS FOR A SUCCESSFUL EVENING

Even when things don't go as planned, the perfect host remains cool-headed and warm-hearted. Try to maximise the time you will spend with your guests by preparing the evening well in advance. Here are a few suggestions:

1. Planning begins with **the invitation**. Think about the combination of guests; who would it be interesting for your guests to meet? It's important to have the correct name, and title, for each of your guests. This is not always evident in the case of couples, so do not take the easy way out by treating a woman as an extension of her husband or partner and only addressing her using his name. Be sure to take the trouble to find out the correct names for both in order to avoid causing offence. And whether you are sending an invitation card or a personalised email invitation it should always include the following: address, starting time, dress code and RSVP details. The perceptive host will be aware of any special requirements, dietary or otherwise, which will avoid the stress of having to come up with a vegetarian or gluten-free meal at the last minute.

2. It is always useful, and essential for formal dinners, to think in advance of the **seating plan**, of how you will arrange your guests around the table. The basic principles are that you alternate men and women, and separate couples. A female guest of honour should be seated to the right of the host, and a male guest of honour to the right of the hostess. At a formal dinner the remaining guests may be seated in order of importance, but, to ensure an easy flow of conversation, guests may also be grouped according to common interests or because they know, or should get to know, each other. Grouping guests to spark new relationships or to put someone in the limelight can be tricky, so it is very satisfying to finally place name cards around the table according to a well thought-out seating plan. It's always helpful to have a copy of the seating plan at the entrance to the dining room, or someone to help the guests find their seats.

3. It's a good idea to plan **the setting** of your event well in advance – background music, flowers, candles. Flowers are the finishing touch on a well-set table. But be careful that they're not too perfumed as certain people have allergies. And watch out for floral arrangements and candelabra that obstruct the view of guests across the table. The colour of the table linen, how the napkins are folded, the china and the glassware all contribute to the ambiance of the table. To decide on a theme and to follow it through is always interesting. If you have paid particular attention to what you will serve your guests, this should be highlighted – an attractive menu card outlining the food and drink to be served can be placed either in the centre of the table (allowing one card for every 4 guests) or an individual card for each guest. When a dinner is being organised for a special event, a personalised menu, in keeping with the event, is often appreciated by your guests as a memento of the occasion.

4. Don't let small **practical problems**, which can rob you of precious time with your guests, get in the way of enjoying your evening. If you have someone to help you in the kitchen or with serving, spend time going through all the details of the menu and what needs to be done so the evening will run smoothly. To be able to depend on professional assistance is worth its weight in gold. Preheated plates are very useful when slow service risks the food becoming cold. Also have an extra place setting or two (cutlery, glasses, china, table napkins, place cards) ready in case of an unexpected guest or an accident when serving. If the tablecloth is accidentally stained, quickly cover the stain with a piece of tin foil and then cover with a table napkin of the same colour. If something is spilled on one of your guest's clothes, offer to have it dry-cleaned.

5. Be mindful that your guests will need to use **the bathroom** at least once over the course of the evening. So, especially when there's a large number, it's a good idea to check or have someone check that it is clean and well-supplied throughout the evening. It is always more tactful not to directly refer to the bathroom but to say something along the lines of 'if you would like to wash your hands …'

6. To avoid too much coming and going, it is useful to have a small serving table or a tray to carry everything you might need. It is also a good idea to put certain items **in the dining room or on the table** in advance – a carafe of water, open bottles of wine, the ice bucket and, of course, the drop-stop (which ensures a drip-free and silent means of pouring wine), as well as bread, butter and salt and pepper. Water glasses should be filled in advance, and if there is going to be a toast make sure that there is wine in the glasses as nothing should be served during the speeches.

7. How best to create a convivial atmosphere and to keep the conversation flowing? You could have a short **speech** ready, which often sets the tone for a successful evening and can add a personal flavour. The host usually gives the first speech. Ideally the speaker should stand up, not just to gain attention, but to add a warmer note to his words. He should raise his glass just above his waist and look at his guests. His speech should last no more than a few minutes, and should end in a toast, where he raises his glass to eye-level and invites his guests to do the same. Any other guest who wishes to say something, should give his speech in the same way.

This is a top Belgian table in the beautiful setting of the Egmont Palace with:

- crystal glasses, candlesticks and vases of **Val Saint Lambert**, collection Kaleido. Val Saint Lambert is purveyor to the Belgian Royal Court and manufacturer since 1826 of unique mouth-blown and hand-cut prestige crystal items. – www.val-saint-lambert.com

- table linen and napkins with a Belgian logo in gold thread, specially made for this book by **Verilin**, with special thanks to Ilse Dedeken. Verilin is a family business from Kortrijk that produces luxury linen products of exceptional quality. – www.verilin.be

- Anzo cutlery designed by Belgian designer Louis de Limburg Stirum for **Eternum**, manufacturer of cutlery and table items for, among others, top hotels around the world. – www.eternum.com

- Limoges porcelain plates hand-turned by Anja Meeusen from **PTZE porcelain**, collection 'Bootje'. – www.ptzeporcelain.com

You should really only clink glasses with your immediate neighbours; it's enough to just raise your glass towards everyone else without the glasses touching. That way you run less of a risk of endangering the crystal.

7 RECOMMENDATIONS FOR A PERFECT TABLE

Hospitality goes hand in hand with a comfortable and harmonious table, a place where your guests can be at ease to enjoy the splendid company and the delicious food. The perfect table should ideally conform to certain rules:

1. **Some geometric rules.** If you have opted for a tablecloth, it should overhang by at least 20 cm (7.87 inch) all around. Napkins are placed either on the plate or to its left. Make sure your guests are not too crowded – allow at least 60-70 cm (23.62-27.56 inch) of personal space for each guest. The absolute minimum between two plates is therefore 30 cm (11.81 inch), which are placed about the width of a thumb from the edge of the table. Observe the same distance from the table's edge for the cutlery which is usually placed in a straight line, even if the forks could also be placed at a diagonal pointing slightly left.

2. **A few rules about left and right.** The cutlery is placed in the order of use, from the outside in. If soup, fish and meat feature on the menu put a soup spoon, a fish knife and a meat knife, going from right to left, to the right of the plate, with blades facing towards the plate. Forks are always placed to the left of the plate. Dessert cutlery, often a spoon or sometimes a small fork with a knife, are placed above the plate, with the handles of the spoon and the knife facing right. If a side plate is being used, it is placed to the left above the plate, with an optional butter knife placed on top.

3. **A few rules about large to small.** Glasses are placed in a straight, or slightly diagonal, line above the plate, from largest (water glass) on the left to smallest (white wine glass) on the right. You can also opt for a triangular arrangement – water glass to the left, white wine glass to the right and red wine glass centred behind. If special beers are served, they should in principle be poured in a wine glass, although refined beer-tasting glasses exist nowadays. If champagne is to be served with dessert, the glass is placed to the left of the water glass.

4. **English or French seating arrangements.** Alas, Europe is not yet united on this matter. The French model places the host and hostess at the centre of the table, facing each other, whereas the English has the host and hostess sitting at either end of the table. Each has its advantages, and it is often the layout of the room, or

seating the host or hostess with a view of the kitchen, which determines which arrangement is most suitable. In both cases the male guest of honour sits to the right of the hostess, and the female guest of honour sits to the right of the host. If opting for the French model, it is worth noting that the cutlery is set with convex surfaces facing upwards, whereas the English place the convex surfaces on the table with the tines of the fork pointing upwards. In both cases, the purpose is to make the hallmark visible.

5. **Serving to the right is the rule.** These days the guest is always served from the right, for plated food and drinks, as well as when the plates are cleared. Remember that food is always served before the wine is poured. Used cutlery is always removed with the plate, to avoid any spattering. The exception to the rule of serving to the right is when the guest has to serve himself from a plate and when he wishes to have another helping, then the serving dish is proffered at his left. Before serving dessert, all the charger plates and cruets are removed. Crumbs are brushed away, or wiped using a napkin. The cheese or dessert plates are then put on the table, and the waiter moves the dessert cutlery to either side of the plate.

6. **Order of service.** The female guest of honour is always served first, followed by the other female guests and finally the hostess. Then the male guests are served in the same order.

7. Make sure you have **finger bowls** (small bowls filled with warm water and a few drops of lemon juice, a slice of lemon or some rose petals) when serving food that is to be eaten by hand. The napkin is used to dry your hands.

PROTOCOL: REACHING OUT TO THE FOUR CORNERS OF THE WORLD

Some tips for the host and hostess

Plan everything: from the invitation, to the menu and the table settings, until the moment your guests arrive.
Always remain calm and friendly.
Rules are there to guide you, not to restrain you, so adapt according to the circumstances.

Some tips for the guest

Try to be punctual and let your host(ess) know if you are delayed or have to leave early. Always bring a small gift. If you have dietary requirements, make them known well in advance. Be guided by the host's customs. Send a thank you message the following day.

Protocol is essentially an extension of the rules of etiquette to take account of dignitaries, who must be received with the necessary and appropriate decorum. At this point, much more formal rules come into play since it is vital to respect each person's rank, often in an international context. Protocol is therefore a job in itself.

When you have the honour to be introduced to such dignitaries, it is useful to bear in mind that you should wait until you are spoken to or are introduced before starting a conversation. When greeting a dignitary, take care to use the correct **form of address** when shaking hands, which differs according to where you are. In general, a king or queen is addressed as 'Your Majesty' on first meeting and thereafter he is addressed as 'Sir' and she as 'Madam'; princes and princesses are addressed as 'Your Royal Highness' and thereafter as 'Sir' or 'Madam'; an Ambassador is addressed as 'Your Excellency' and a government minister as 'Minister'. It is probably best to be advised on the exact form of address to be used in advance of any meeting.

Also, in an increasingly globalised world, we need to constantly adjust our manners and to be aware of the nuances of **different customs and cultural sensitivities**. Here are a few examples:

In certain cultures you should pay particular attention to the feet, which are regarded as unclean. You should therefore be careful not to sit with the soles of your feet, or the soles of your shoes, showing, and you should avoid using your foot to point at something. You also need to take care with your hands. In certain cultures it is disrespectful to use your index finger to point, so it is safer to keep your hands open when using them to explain something. In cultures which forbid men and women to shake hands, you can place your right hand lightly on your chest and incline your head slightly saying 'I am delighted to meet you'. In Muslim countries and in parts of India the left hand is regarded as impure, so it is best to use the right hand. It is sometimes preferable, particularly in certain Asian countries, to offer gifts with both hands, and in the same way to use both hands to offer and accept business cards. Some cultures are very lax about punctuality, whereas others are very precise. In certain places it is considered rude to eat everything on your plate, whereas in others it's the highest compliment you can pay your host. To conclude, you should go with the flow and constantly adapt to the situation.

.be our guest

---

7 cocktails and 3 appetizers

PRE-DINNER, THE BELGIAN WAY

Jan Vandenplas

This talented mixologist, a young bartender at Bar Nine in Leuven, serves an array of delicious cocktails using some of Belgium's best ingredients. Although Belgium is world-renowned for its beer, it is increasingly establishing itself in the realm of spirits, and is skillfully distilling award-winning vodkas, gins and whiskies. But other local drinks and ingredients also lend themselves perfectly to surprising cocktails … – **www.bar-nine.be**

7 delicious Belgian Cocktails by **Jan Vandenplas**, winner of the 18th edition of the Stella Artois World Draught Master.

Sipping a cocktail is an exploration of flavours, a journey where a touch of the exotic sets you dreaming of places faraway. With or without alcohol, a sophisticated cocktail is an experience in itself, a bespoke luxury, prepared with love for a special moment. Serving your guests a cocktail is the ultimate expression of hospitality. The possibility of presenting something created just for him or her will immediately induce the feeling of being a 'very special guest'. What a perfect way to start your party or dinner in style!

Where do our spirits come from?
The story of spirits 'made in Belgium' began with the return of the Crusaders. Although there are indications that the Chinese had already mastered the art of distillation and that the Greeks and Romans had succeeded in making liqueurs from wine, the invention of distillation is generally attributed to the Arabs, who ascribed medicinal properties to alcohol. Slowly but surely, in the 16th century, news of this new concoction spread across Europe and it gained in popularity. **Jenever**, also known as Dutch gin, soon made its appearance. Cereal-based and often flavoured with juniper berries, from which it takes its name, the North Sea fishermen were among its earliest enthusiasts. British soldiers became acquainted with 'jenever' during the Thirty Years' War and, due to brisk trade with the Low Countries, it made its way to London. It immediately caught on, infused with herbs more in tune with local tastes, and was eventually simply known as gin, an abbreviation of its original name.

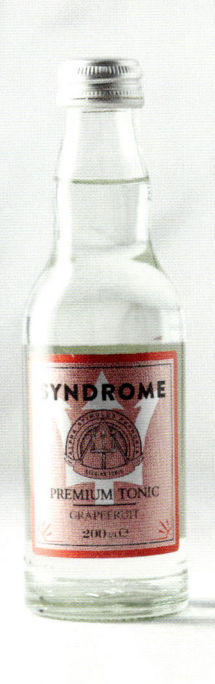

Elderflower Kir

This cocktail is ideal for those who love sparkling wine or champagne with a little extra something. Golden, sparkling and with a hint of fruit, this cocktail is less sweet than the classic 'Kir Royal', and appreciated by both young and old. It is easy to prepare, so it's the perfect drink when hosting large numbers.

Ingredients
4 cl (1.35 fl oz) Belfleur Elderflower (liqueur)
12 cl (4 fl oz) Ruffus Chardonnay Brut (sparkling wine)

Belfleur Elderflower is inspired by the ancient Belgian tradition of homemade elderflower drinks, which are reputed to have medicinal properties. The delicate flavours of this liqueur provide a 'summer in your glass' feel suitable for a wide range of cocktails. – www.fdwbrands.com

The outstanding internationally acclaimed 'Cuvée Ruffus', produced by Vignobles des Agaises, is undoubtedly the pride of Belgian sparkling wines. It is a 100% Chardonnay 'Blanc de Blancs', cultivated in vineyards with rich limestone soil. Lay it down for 12 months and its delicious bubbles will be impatient to fill your glass. – www.ruffus.be

To prepare
Pour the liqueur into a champagne glass and top with chilled sparkling wine. Garnish with a sprig of mint or, in summer, a lime wedge.

DID YOU KNOW

- The elderflower liqueur in this cocktail can be replaced by another liqueur of your choice. There are many distillers in Belgium producing artisanal liqueurs, including herbal 'elixirs' with a pronounced aniseed flavour, whose medicinal properties are supposedly effective against gastrointestinal disturbances and insomnia. Apparently they're very effective, because many horse breeders in Belgium keep a bottle in their stables, and if a horse whose digestive tract is blocked drinks a bottle of it ... all is clear.

- As a general rule, kir is made with dry (brut) champagne (kir royale), but a semi-dry (demi-sec) or a light dry white wine can also be used, and it is then called a 'Kir Vin Blanc'. The classification brut, sec and demi-sec indicates the increasing sugar level of the wine. So you should adjust the amount of liqueur used depending on the type of wine.

- A champagne glass or flute has a thin wall so as not to affect the temperature of the champagne; within seconds a thin glass will adopt the temperature of the liquid.

A Monastic Gin & Tonic

Whoever states that gin and tonic is an ordinary cocktail, definitely didn't try this Belgian hipster version! The surprising addition of bitter brown abbey beer balances and even neutralises the bitterness of the gin and tonic. The result is a very sophisticated cocktail that will appeal to all your guests.

Ingredients
5 cl (1.7 fl oz) Strange Donkey Wintergin
6 cl (2 fl oz) Syndrome Premium Tonic – Raw
6 cl (2 fl oz) Orval

This Antwerp artisanal gin distillery won a gold medal with its limited edition Wintergin. With Yuzu as its main ingredient, this gin offers refreshing citrus tones with a subtle touch of Japanese herbs, shiso, cherry blossom and some local herbs. – www.strangedonkeygin.com

This is the only brand of tonic produced in Belgium. Syndrome Premium Tonic – Raw combines the natural ingredients of Buddha's Hand (an aromatic lemon variety) and raw Cinchona bark extracts in a harmonised and challenging palette. The natural quinine leaves a long bitter aftertaste. – www.syndrometonic.be

With its characteristic bitter fruity taste, Orval beer is a benchmark in the exclusive world of authentic Trappist beers. The Orval brewery's activities are still governed by the monastic community, who ensure that a percentage of their revenue goes to charity. – www.orval.be

To prepare
Fill the glass to the brim with ice cubes. Pour in the gin and tonic and stir well. Top with the beer and add a zest of lemon for freshness. Cheers!

DID YOU KNOW

- Each gin has its own perfect garnish and mixer (tonic) – this is called the 'Perfect Serve'. If the garnish is a lime, lemon or grapefruit wedge, put it in first, before pouring the tonic. However, if you use a dry garnish, such as juniper berries or cinnamon sticks, add them at the last minute.

- Both a tulip glass and a tall glass are suitable to serve gin and tonic. The tall glass can be completely filled with ice, which guarantees a well chilled and more sparkling cocktail. A tulip glass will enhance more sophisticated flavours, especially when adding a special garnish.

- Mixing gin and tonic goes back to British colonial times in India. The settlers had to take their daily shot of quinine to protect themselves against malaria, as was the case in the former Belgian Congo, where quinine plantations were also set up. The British dissolved quinine in sweetened sodas, and thus created 'Indian Tonic'. Subsequently they mixed it with their beloved gin. And so the famous gin and tonic was born!

- Besides the exceptional Strange Donkey Wintergin, you will find in Belgium a wide variety of excellent and original gins, such as 1836 Organic Gin, Belgin, Blind Tiger, Buss N° 509, Clover, Copperhead, Crazy Monday, Duingin, Filliers, Forest, Ginderella, Ground Control, HenTho, La Petite Merveille, Marula, Matterhorn, Spring, Vibe …

Nosy Nose

This is Jan Vandenplas' signature mocktail, full of childhood memories and flavours. You can find cuberdons, also called 'neuzekes' (little noses) in Flanders or 'chapeaux de curé' (priest's hats) in Wallonia, at almost every local Belgian market. The appeal of these traditional Belgian sweets is the subtle contrast between its smooth crisp shell and its juicy centre of sweet raspberry syrup. When you bite it, the crust shell bursts open and an explosion of flavours tickles your tongue. The Nosy Nose, with its refreshing aftertaste, is a real treat for fans of alcohol-free cocktails.

DID YOU KNOW

- The unique and inimitable taste of cuberdon syrup will also enhance your desserts. Homemade cuberdon syrup is prepared as follows: Melt 1 kilo (2 lbs 3 oz) cuberdons in 1 liter (1 quart) of water on a low heat while stirring. Cool and put it in a sealed bottle in the refrigerator. Couldn't be simpler.

- According to legend the cuberdon has its origins in the 19th century and was created by a clergyman from Bruges, which seems to be confirmed by etymology. In an older version of Flemish spoken in Bruges, 'kuper' referred to a 'cone', the shape of the cuberdon. In Flanders the gallicized name 'cuberdon' is rarely used. This heavenly confection is sold over the counter as 'neuzeke' (little noze), 'tsoepke', 'topneus' (nose tip), 'topke' (little peak), and many other pet names. The recipe for cuberdons is one of the best kept secrets in the Kingdom of Belgium, with only a few select artisans still using it to make the perfect cuberdon, which is a recognised Flemish regional product.

- One of the essential ingredients of the cuberdons is arabic gum. This precious gum is extracted from the acacia tree, mainly in sub-Saharan Africa. Because of the scarcity of arabic gum during World War II, the cuberdon was very nearly consigned to oblivion. Fortunately, once the gum became available again in 1946, those who had safeguarded its secret were able to start producing it again.

Ingredients
2 cl (1.7 fl oz) Leopold cuberdon syrup
2 cl (1.7 fl oz) lime juice
10 cl (3.4 fl oz) Ritchie Grapefruit (lemonade)

Cuberdons Léopold, named after the first King of Belgium, are unmistakably the crown jewels of Belgian cuberdons. It says on the box: 'Prepared with love in the Kingdom of Belgium'. You can almost feel the love in the exquisite taste of these cuberdons, still made using the original 19th century recipe.
– www.cuberdonsleopold.com

Happiness bottled! Ritchie is an original Belgian 'vintage' lemonade that was recently given a new sparkling life. Pleasantly bubbly, with a fresh grapefruit flavour and a hint of pineapple, this hipster drink will catapult you into the swinging fifties!
– www.drinkritchie.com

To prepare
Fill a big glass with crushed ice, add the lime juice, cuberdon syrup and then the lemonade. Stir until the syrup is well dissolved and garnish with a frozen cuberdon, which makes an original and delicious ice cube.

Rocking Raspberry

Raspberries are as much a joy for the eyes as for the mouth, with their shades of pink and red, and their delicate taste and texture. Think of them as vitamin C in a fresh fruit format! Many varieties are grown in Belgium, especially in the province of Limburg, its biggest fruit region. Jan's giddy signature cocktail will improve your mood – it might even make you ecstatic – ready for a most enjoyable evening.

Ingredients

5 cl (1.7 fl oz) BUSS N° 509 Raspberry gin
2 cl (0.7 fl oz) sugar syrup
2 cl (0.7 fl oz) lime juice
2 cl (0.7 fl oz) raspberry coulis
1 egg
10 cl (3.4 fl oz) Syndrome Premium Tonic – Grapefruit

This award winning brand produces fruity gins under the BUSS N° 509 series brand, all artisan and made in Belgium with fresh raspberries and fine herbs, with no added sugar, artificial flavours or colouring agents. – www.buss509.com

This Belgian tonic is a refreshing drink with a very low sugar content and a pleasant aroma. It has a slight resemblance to bitter lemon but with a pronounced grapefruit flavour. www.syndrometonic.be

To prepare

Dissolve 1 kilo (2 lbs 3 oz) of sugar in a saucepan with ½ liter (2 cups) of water. Stir over a low heat until the syrup is clear. Allow to cool and store in a sealed bottle in the fridge. Put the gin, sugar syrup, lime juice, raspberry coulis and egg white into a cocktail shaker with some ice and shake for 20 seconds. Pour through a strainer into the glass and immediately add the tonic. Garnish with lime zest, a sprig of mint and a fresh raspberry.

DID YOU KNOW

- Raspberries contain a lot of vitamin C and other antioxidants. Some even claim that eating a lot of raspberries is a proven anti-aging cure. This will make you ready to rock the house!
Because raspberries are composed of many miniature fruits around a hollow core, they contain a lot of fibre which is beneficial for keeping you regular!

- Preparing your own raspberry coulis for this cocktail is definitely worth it. It's not only healthy, it also adds flavour. Mix 1 kilo (5 cups) of sugar in a saucepan with ½ kilo (1lbs) of raspberries. Allow to simmer for a few minutes over low heat until the berries are soft.

Belgian Mojito

Ernest Hemingway would undoubtedly love this Belgian version of the traditional Cuban mojito. By using gin as the main ingredient, this classic cocktail becomes even more delicious and gains in character.

Ingredients
4 cl (1.4 fl oz) Smeets Extra Hasseltse Graanjenever (Dutch gin)
1 cl (0.35 fl oz) HAVN HAV rum
2 cl (0.7 fl oz) passion fruit syrup
2 cl (0.7 fl oz) passion fruit juice
6 cl (2 fl oz) Hoegaarden
Lime wedges, ½ lime and 12-15 mint leaves

Among the approximately 400 Belgian jenever brands, Smeets Extra Hasseltse graanjenever *is one of the most emblematic. Distilled according to a centuries-old tradition, this 35° jenever has a full-bodied flavour after a minimum of 6 months of ageing in barrels with the added juniper extracts.*
– www.smeets.be

HAVN is a delicious rum made in Belgium. One of its four flavour varieties has been inspired by the Spanish archipelago around Havana. HAVN HAV has a pronounced taste of raw cocoa and mandarin, as well as a gentle hint of vanilla.
– www.havn.com

Hoegaarden is the most famous white beer in Belgium and perhaps in the world. It is a fresh thirst-quenching beer with distinctive notes of coriander and orange peel.
– www.hoegaarden.be

To prepare
Bring 250 ml (1 cup) of passion fruit pulp, the same amount of water, 20 ml (0.7 fl oz) of lemon juice and 500 g (2.5 cups) of sugar to the boil and let it simmer on medium heat for 3 minutes until you have a clear syrup. Allow to cool and strain through a muslin. Store in a sealed bottle in the fridge.
Muddle the lime wedges in the glass to release the juice. Rub the mint leaves against the palm of your hand so that their veins release the aromas. Add the mint leaves to the glass and half-fill with crushed ice. Pour the gin, rum, passion fruit syrup and juice over it and stir well. Fill the glass with more ice and top off with Hoegaarden. Garnish with passion fruit and a sprig of mint. If you prefer your mojito less sweet, you can leave out the passion fruit syrup.

DID YOU KNOW

◆ The French have cognac, the Scots have whisky and the Belgians have jenever, one of the oldest spirits in Europe. There are still about 25 distilleries, such as Bruggeman, Daens, De Stoop, Distillerie de Biercée, Filliers, Peket de Wallonie, Peterman, Smeets, Wilderen, Wortegemse ... and even a jenever museum in Hasselt. Have you heard of the Flemish term 'flessengeluk' ('luck of the bottle')? When people used to order jenever as a digestif, it was poured into a small glass until it was at the point of overflowing so that the only way to drink it was to bend over and sip from the glass. If there was not enough left in the bottle to fill the glass in this way, you were said to have 'the luck of the bottle' because you didn't have to pay for your drink.

◆ Rum is often associated with pirates, Caribbean beaches and tall stories, which is not entirely without reason. Distilling alcohol from sugar cane goes back a long way, but rum as we know it today is a recipe from the seventeenth century, when the Caribbean slaves discovered that molasses could be fermented into alcohol. It is true that rum was a pirate drink. On many ships it was common to have a daily tot of rum to keep the spirits up.

◆ 'Mixing beers' is very common in Belgium. Many simple variations exist such as 'Mazout' (beer and Cola), 'Snow White' (beer and Sprite), 'Tango' (dark beer and grenadine), 'Smurfs Beer' (beer and Blue Curacao), which are very popular among students. More sophisticated cocktails with a touch of beer have become increasingly popular in recent years.

◆ Did they have too much free time on their hands, were they tired of altar wine, or was it divine inspiration? Unfortunately, we can no longer ask the monks of Hoegaarden, but what is certain is that it was these monks who first came up with the recipe for white beer around 1445.

Belgian Horse's Neck

This elegant cocktail has existed since 1890 and is an American classic. The obligatory long strip of lemon peel which swirls inside the glass reminds us of a horse's neck and gives it its name. As it was the favourite drink of Ian Fleming, James Bond regularly sips this golden concoction. This is a simple but hearty cocktail that warms you from the moment it touches your lips.

DID YOU KNOW

- Whisky is a drink distilled from fermented grain mash that has aged for at least three years in oak barrels. There are several different grades of whisky. At the bottom of the ladder there is *grain* whisky, made with unmalted cereals and produced on an industrial scale, with a relatively flat taste. It is mainly used in *blended* whiskies, a mix of *grain* and *malt* whiskies. The latter is made from a fermented mash consisting primarily of malted barley. *Blended* whiskies are by far the largest group available on the market. The pure malt whisky, also called *blended malt* whisky, is the cream of the crop, the result of uniform ripening of malted barley without additives. And when the label mentions '*single malt* whisky', it means that the whisky comes from a single distillery with its own characteristics. This category includes the acclaimed 'The Belgian Owl', which is among the top 10 in the world. Other great Belgian whiskies include Goldlys, Kempisch Vuur, Lambertus, Rye Whiskey, Wild Weasel ...

- Whisky can be drunk neat, diluted with water (even a drop opens up the taste) and/or with ice cubes. The latter is called *on the rocks* because the Scots originally used stones from the river bed to cool their whisky.

- There is no whisky tradition in Belgium although both beer and whisky are made from grain. However, in recent years an interesting synergy has developed: Belgian whisky brewers are making clever use of the malt mash processed by their colleagues in the breweries, for example Duvel Distilled, Gouden Carolus ... In this way, the tradition of beer brewing and the recent phenomenon of distilling whisky are combined, resulting in whiskies with a unique Belgian character.

Ingredients
5 cl (1.7 fl oz) of Belgian Owl Whisky
10 cl (3.4 fl oz) ginger ale or lemonade
2 dashes angostura bitters
Long spiral of lemon peel

With its numerous international awards, The Belgian Owl is undeniably the best Belgian single malt whisky. Light, creamy and fresh, with notes of vanilla, persimmon, pear and a hint of unripe banana, this delicate reserved whisky is almost too refined to be used in a cocktail. – www.belgianwhisky.com

To prepare
Place a long spiral of lemon peel inside a tall glass and fill it up with crushed ice. Pour over the whisky and two dashes of angostura bitters liquor. Finish with ginger ale or tasty lemonade.

Sweet Diamond

This is another of Jan's signature cocktails. He calls this one 'candy crush'. By soaking his favourite candies – gummy bears – in alcohol in the freezer for 24 hours, he gets jelly shot bears to use as a garnish. But once he forgot about his gummy bears and left them too long in the freezer, and they ended up completely dissolved. And so a delicious vodka cocktail was born!

Ingredients

5 cl (1.7 fl oz) Cosmik Pure Diamond (Vodka)
2 cl (0.7 fl oz) passion fruit or other fruit syrup
12 cl (4 fl oz) Syndrome Rose Lemonade
250 g (1 ¼ cup) gummies (bears or others) per litre of vodka

Cosmik Pure Diamond (37.5°) is a Belgian premium vodka ranked among the 10 best vodkas in the world. This multiple award winning vodka undergoes six distillations, resulting in a smooth blend of woody aromas and unrivalled softness. www.distal.be

Syndrome Rose Lemonade is a real taste explosion! The Bulgarian rose extract gives the sweet notes of this soft drink an elegant and almost royal taste. Equally delicious and refreshing to drink as it is. – www.buss-spirits.be

To prepare

Make an infused vodka the day before by mixing 175 g (6.2 oz) of your favourite gummies with a bottle of Kosmik Pure Diamond vodka (700 ml (3 cups)). Heat carefully to 60 °C (140 °F), being mindful that alcohol evaporates at 70 °C (158 °F), while stirring constantly until the gummies are completely dissolved. Set aside to cool. Store in the fridge in a sealed bottle.

Pour all the ingredients into the glass and fill it up with crushed ice. Garnish with a *mexican elbow*, a small ice bowl made by putting crushed ice in a mexican elbow lemon squeezer. Garnish with some gummies.

DID YOU KNOW

- Vodka – a Slavic word for water – is the most neutral type of distilled spirit, both in flavour and colour. It can be made from different kinds of raw materials, ranging from potatoes and quinoa to various types of grain. The Poles and the Russians are still quarrelling about who made the first vodka.

- Vodka is the perfect mixer for all kinds of juices and drinks. For that reason many classic cocktails are vodka-based, including the 'Screwdriver' (the one and only vodka-orange), the 'Sling' (with sugar syrup and lemon juice) and the 'Bloody Mary' (with tomato juice).

Dimitry and Aagje were writing their future in the stars when they decided on a name for their restaurant in the former Roman stronghold of Tongeren, because 'Magis' is the Latin word for 'more'. And from the moment they finished their studies, this atypical gastronomic duo have set their sights on achieving ever more. Together, they pursued Dimitry's culinary passion and worked tirelessly to reach the top. Today, in a 14th century building that once belonged to the German Knights of Alden Biesen, they offer a 'magical' cuisine with a modern approach that's based on global experience. – www.restaurantmagis.be

Chef Lysens has prepared three simple Belgian appetizers with a twist, and a nod to the **Consulate-General of Belgium in Guangzhou, China**.

Dimitry Lysens and Aagje Moens

From autodidact to magical star team

serves 4

Nasturtium with shrimp milk

The 3000-year-old Chinese philosophy of 'Feng Shui' teaches how environmental elements can influence happiness. Water, one of the five elements, is very important for harmony in life. So let this floating amuse-bouche contribute to a harmonious and welcoming start to the evening!

100 g (3.5 oz) grey shrimp heads // 1 bay leaf // 1 sprig thyme // 5 lovage leaves // ½ clove garlic // 200 ml (7 fl oz) milk // 1 sheet gelatine // 8 nasturtium leaves with stalk

Bring all the ingredients, except the gelatine, to the boil and allow to simmer for 15 minutes. Strain and mix with the previously soaked gelatine. Allow to cool and blend until smooth.
Fill the nasturtium leaves with the shrimp milk and put them to float in a dish filled with water and pebbles.

Serves 4

Mini Peking duck skewers

There are not many dishes that are based on an imperial family tree that is more than 700 years old. According to the official Beijing website, Peking duck dates back to the time of the Yuan Dynasty (1271 to 1368) when the Mongol Emperors ruled China. Chef Lysens makes his own mini version of this delicacy.

1 duck leg // 50 ml (1.7 fl oz) of soy sauce // 40 g (1.4 oz) of sake // 1 star anise // 10 g (0.35 oz) ginger // 1 garlic clove // 1 red pepper // ½ stick of cinnamon // 50 ml (1.7 fl oz) cider vinegar // 500 ml (1 pint) water // 4 twigs (or wooden sticks) // white and black sesame seeds

Slowly bring all the ingredients to the boil in a small covered saucepan. The duck leg should be at least ¾ submerged in the liquid. Put the saucepan in an oven preheated to 160 °C (320 °F) for about 1 ½ hours until the duck is tender. Carefully remove the meat from the liquid and allow to cool.
Pass the liquid through a sieve and cook until reduced to a thick sauce with a strong taste. Cut the duck leg into 2-3 cm (0.8 – 1.2 inch) cubes and quickly fry the skin side until crisp. Cover the meat with the sauce, sprinkle with sesame seeds and make a mini-skewer.

Serves 4

Red and yellow devils
Yellow and red beetroot, black toast, trout mousse

In the world of sport, the Red Devils are undeniably world ambassadors for Belgium. Hence an amusing yet tasty snack in their honour.

2 red beetroots // 2 yellow beetroots // 20 g (0.7 oz) sugar // 50 ml (1.7 fl oz) vinegar // 150 ml (5 fl oz) water // 1 g (15 gr) salt // 50 g (1.8 oz) trout fillet // 50 g (1.8 oz) cream // 50 g (1.8 oz) fish stock // 1 sheet of gelatine // 20 g (0.7 oz) trout roe // 4 slices of black toast

Mix the sugar, water, vinegar and salt and bring to the boil. Finely slice one beetroot of each colour. Put the yellow slices into the boiling liquid and cook for 1 minute. Remove, and then add the red slices and also cook for 1 minute. Allow to cool.

Heat the fish stock and add the previously soaked gelatine, stirring to dissolve. Process the trout fillet and the stock in a blender until smooth. Pass through a fine sieve. Allow to cool for a few minutes. Using a spatula, add the lightly whipped cream. Leave to cool in the refrigerator.

Cut the remaining beetroots in half and using an apple corer make three cylindrical holes in each. Use the boiled beet slices to make little cones, fill them with the trout mousse and place them in the small holes. Garnish with the trout roe and serve with a slice of black toast.

Guangzhou

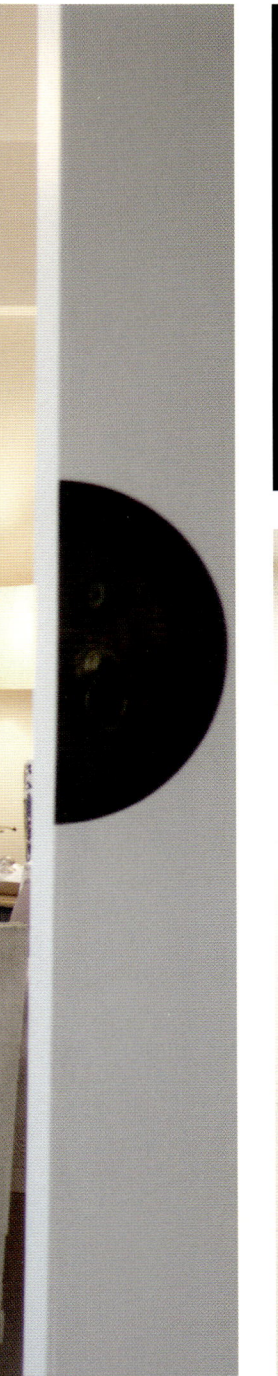

Belgian wine, an ambassador in the making

.be our guest

Whether or not global warming has anything to do with it, these days it's not unusual to pass a vineyard when taking a walk in the Belgian countryside. After centuries of lying dormant, Belgian viticulture seems to have really taken off.

The notion of wine in Belgium may surprise you, but it's not new. The Romans are said to have planted Belgium's first vines. What's certain, is that abbeys already produced wine in the Carolingian era around Ghent and Liège. The nobility and wealthy bourgeoisie caught on to the trend and, from the 13th century onwards, vineyards regularly appear in sales deeds, wills and tax registers. Around the 16th century, viticulture declined due to foreign imports of wine, the devastation caused by religious wars and the noticeably colder climate (just look at Breughel's winter landscapes). So, apart from a few surviving vineyards, the vines disappeared and wine production died out.

It was not until the 1960's that wine-making was revived and has grown apace, especially over the past ten years, during which Belgian wine production has increased fivefold. A more favourable climate, in combination with the introduction of better-stocked grape varieties, has contributed to the growth of Belgian wines. But above all, it is the expertise and commitment of an increasing number of professional and semi-professional wine growers that has improved the quality of the wines. Because of the relatively cool climate, white and sparkling wines are predominant (more than 80% of Belgian viticulture). According to some, the future lies mainly with 'bubbles'. Even so, a number of excellent red wines are being produced. Meanwhile, the European Union has officially recognised Belgium as a wine-producing country, to the satisfaction of more than 200 Belgian winemakers. And this interest in viticulture goes beyond our borders; many successful Belgian wine initiatives can be noted, among others, in France, Spain, Italy, Austria and even in South Africa and Australia.

Below are some suggestions for excellent, award-winning Belgian wines to grace your table.

Aldeneyck

Aldeneyck
Aldeneyck consistently produces top wines with a beautiful minerality. www.wijndomein-aldeneyck.be

[red] **Pinot noir**: a dry, powerful, lightly-oaked wine with black cherry and wild blackberry notes – serve with cheese, red meat, stew and game
[white] **Chardonnay Heerenlaak**: dry, full-bodied oaked wine, full of character – serve with baked poultry, oriental cuisine, pasta, shellfish and fish
[white] **Pinot Gris**: dry, fresh, fruity,slightly smoky wine with spicy notes – serve as an aperitif, with poultry, shellfish and fish
[sparkling] **Pinot Brut**: expressive nose of fruit and fruit blossom – serve as an aperitif, with shellfish and simple fish dishes

Chardonnay Meerdael

Chardonnay Meerdael
This multi-award winning wine estate is the pioneer of Belgian sparkling wines. www.chardonnaymeerdael.be

[sparkling] **Chardonnay Brut**: aroma of spring blossom, ripe fruit with a slightly exotic touch – serve as an aperitif, with shellfish

Chateau Bon Baron

Chateau Bon Baron
This wine estate is one of the few that specializes in versatile red wines. www.chateaubonbaron.be

[red] **Pinot Noir**: dry, powerful wine, full of character, soft red fruit and vanilla notes – serve with barbecued meats, charcuterie, poultry, foie gras, pasta, red meat
[red] **Pinot Noir Trésor**: dry, powerful wine, full of character, red fruit and vanilla notes – serve with poultry, cheese, red meat, game, stews
[red] **La Grande Trésor**: dry wine, full of character, full red and black berry notes,woody spicy aroma – serve with charcuterie, red meat, game, stews
[white] **Pinot blanc**: dry wine, full of character, subtle tropical fruit aromas, floral notes and a light spiciness – serve with asparagus, poultry, mussels, fish

Château de Bioul

Château de Bioul
A true chateau producing sophisticated white wines with the utmost respect for the environment. This beautiful domain attracts many visitors with its wine tourism tour.
www.chateaudebioul.be

[white] **Batte de la Reine**: wine with expressive floral and lychee aromas – serve with warm goat's cheese, cheese fondue, fish, white meat, poultry with tarragon sauce
[white] **Terre Charlotte**: elegant wine with a feminine touch – with asparagus and soft, creamy as well as hard cheeses

Clos d'Opleeuw
This small but renowned producer benefits from a unique microclimate due to its walled vineyard. The wines have a strong reputation which extends far beyond the Belgian borders, and can hold their own against the great Bordeaux wines. www.clos-d-opleeuw.be

[white] **Chardonnay**: a dry wine, full of character, very fruity with hints of honey, butter, yellow plums, ripe apple and vanilla – serve with poultry, cheese, fish in cream sauce

Domaine du Chant d'Éole
A newcomer, named after the windmills of the region. These two sparkling wines received immediate recognition and are extremely popular. www.chantdeole.be

[sparkling] **Chant d'Eole brut**: based on a Chardonnay with a light touch of Pinot Blanc, traditional method – serve as an aperitif
[sparkling] **Chant d'Eole brut rosé**: a fruity aroma of red berries with a pale pink-orange colour – serve as an aperitif, with dessert

Domaine du Chenoy
This interesting wine estate in the heart of the province of Namur was one of the first professional wine domains in Wallonia. www.domaine-du-chenoy.com

[sparkling] **La Perle de Wallonie**: traditional method, with a subtle perfume of aubergine flowers and a hint of citrus fruits – serve as an aperitif
[wine liqueur] **Muscat Bleu**: blackcurrant and cherry aromas – perfect with chocolate desserts

Domaine de Mellemont
This vineyard is the pioneer of the new wine-growing trend in Wallonia and produces the favourite wine of chef Sang Hoon Degeimbre. www.domaine-de-mellemont.com

[red] **Pinot Noir**: develops delicate cherry aromas – with poultry, red meats and game birds
[sparkling] **Bulles pour elle**: traditional method with soft bubbles, favourite of Justine Henin, former world tennis champion – serve as an aperitif
[white] **Cuvée du Verger des Moines**: spicy notes, citrus and muscat – serve with poultry, mushrooms

Entre-deux-Monts
The wines of this estate, the third largest in Belgium, regularly receive awards, including, more recently, for their red wine. These wines are appreciated by many enthusiasts, both at home and abroad. www.entre-deux-monts.be

[white] **Pinot Gris**: aromas of ripe fruit, honey and sweet spices – serve with poultry, shellfish, salads, fish
[red] **Pinot Noir**: fruity red wine with soft tannins – serve with charcuterie, beef carpaccio, chicken, steak tartare, tomato dishes, cheese
[sparkling] **Wiscoutre**: very fresh and fruity wine – serve as an aperitif, with dessert

Gloire de Duras
This walled vineyard has a microclimate that ensures high quality wines. www.gloirededuras.be

[white] **Chardonnay-Auxerrois**: floral, fruity, spicy aromas – serve as an aperitif, with poultry, fish

Kitsberg
This family business produces very accessible white wines, including a Chardonnay which has won gold for several years in a row. www.kitsberg.be

[white] **Chardonnay Krachtig**: hints of honey, pear and fresh butter – serve as an aperitif, with poultry, fish
[white] **Pinot Gris**: a wine that is graceful or robust depending on the season, with a herbal bouquet and white fruit notes – serve with poultry, fish, cheese, dessert
[white] **Pinot Blanc 'Cuvée V'**: fresh and fruity with notes of apples and white fruit – serve as an aperitif, with fish, white meat

Kluisberg
This is the largest wine estate of the Hageland with excellent value for quality wines. www.kluisberg.be

[white] **Pinot Blanc**: dry, fresh and fruity wine with a pleasant spiciness – serve as an aperitif, with shellfish, salad
[white] **Pinot Gris**: dry, fresh and yellow-fruity wine – serve as an aperitif, with Asian food, shellfish

Clos d'Opleeuw

Domaine du Chant d'Éole

Domaine du Chenoy

Domaine de Mellemont

Entre-deux-Monts

Gloire de Duras

Kitsberg

Kluisberg

Schorpion

Vignoble des Agaises

Vin de Liège

Wijnkasteel Genoels-Elderen

Wijndomein Hoenshof

Wijnkasteel Haksberg

Schorpion
Only 200 km from the Champagne region, Schorpion focuses on sparkling wines. It is one of the best known and best sparkling wines in the country. www.schorpion.com

[sparkling] **Black brut**: fruity with apricot, yeast and brioche aromas – serve as an aperitif, with shellfish, salad

Vignoble des Agaises
This vineyard close to the French border produces the best Belgian sparkling wines, and attracts many visitors. Regular winners of gold and silver medals at international competitions, these high quality wines are usually sold out before they even reach the market, and deserve to be known as the champagne of Belgium. www.ruffus.be

[sparkling] **Ruffus Chardonnay Brut** and **Ruffus Chardonnay Brut Sauvage** are both very refined in taste, with perfect bubbles and fruity aromas complemented by a perfect balance of minerality

Vin de Liège
This remarkable crowdfunding project puts the viticulture of Liège back on the map and successfully engages in winemaking in a socially and environmentally sustainable manner. www.vindeliege.be

[white] **Contrepoint**: a powerful complex wine with hints of nuts, melon and pear – serve with white meat, fish
[white] **Ô the Craie**: a complex wine with hints of yellow fruit – serve with fish, seafood, poultry, goat's cheese

Wijnkasteel Genoels-Elderen
This is probably the best known, and largest, Belgian wine producer. The wines feature on the menus of many top chefs. The beautiful chateau and surrounding parklands also attract many visitors. www.wijnkasteel.com

[white] **Chardonnay Blue**: a fruity aromatic wine – serve as an aperitif, with light dishes such as asparagus or oysters
[sparkling] **Silver Pearl**: a wine with a smoky dimension and fruity aromas – serve as an aperitif, with shellfish, fish
[sparkling] **Black Pearl**: a wine with nutty tones and exotic fruit aromas – serve as an aperitif, with shellfish, fish, dessert

Wijndomein Hoenshof
This wine estate produces aromatic, accessible wines, which regularly take home the prize for best Belgian wine. Recently, a number of interesting ice wines have been added to the range, based on grapes, apples or pears. www.puurwijn.be

[red] **Cuvée Hoenshof**: a dry, powerful wine, full of character – serve with barbecued meats, pasta, red meat, stews, game
[white] **Chardonnay Barrique**: a dry, very fruity wine, full of character – serve as an aperitif, with cheese, shellfish, fish, poultry
[white] **Cuvée Pinot**: a dry, very fruity wine, full of character – serve as an aperitif, with shellfish, fish, poultry
[white] **Würzer**: a sweet white wine with good acidity – serve with dessert, Asian food

Wijnkasteel Haksberg
This is a promising young eco-friendly wine estate which immediately hit the mark with one of its white wines. The name of each wine refers to (the Latin name of) a bird that can be spotted on the estate. www.haksberg.be

[white] **Virido**: a fruity wine with flower and stone-fruit aromas – serve with fruity desserts, light vegetable dishes, fish, poultry
[red] **Rocopo**: a powerful wine with dark fruity notes, woody and smoky aromas – serve with stews, small game, pasta with rich meat sauce

www.belgianwines.com
www.lesvinsbelges.be

.be our guest

7 top chefs

CREATE A MENU FOR
21 EMBASSIES OF BELGIUM

Full of dynamism and creativity, chef Maxime Collard has definitely put the Belgian Ardennes on the map. Born and raised in this beautiful region of forests and hills, with an abundance of wildlife and freshwater fish, his cooking maintains the perfect balance between his passion for the terroir and for contemporary cuisine with an international edge. His elegant, award-winning restaurant, '**La Table de Maxime**', is located in Our, a typical Ardennes village, nestled in a loop of the river to which it owes its name, which is said to be one of the most beautiful rural hamlets in Wallonia.
www.maximecollard.be

The talented Collard took inspiration for his menu from the **Embassies of Belgium in Budapest** (Hungary), **Canberra** (Australia) and **Pretoria** (South-Africa).

Maxime Collard

A taste of the soul of the Ardennes

Budapest (HUNGARY)
Starter: Goose liver Maxime's way
If there is one mouth-watering specialty from Hungary that is rarely absent from festive dinner tables, it must be goose liver. Chef Maxime has created a deliciously colourful dish to do justice to this ingredient, which is Hungary's national pride, by combining surprising textures, sweet and salty tones, as well as vegetables and herbs from his own garden.

Pretoria (SOUTH-AFRICA)
Main dish: Kudu of the Ardennes forests
There is no shortage of game either in South Africa or in the Ardennes forests. Wild boar, deer and mouflon – distant relative of the South African Kudu – are hunted in season and are paid a final tribute by horns blowing in alternating tones. With his preparation of fillet of young deer, which he combines with our much beloved gingerbread ('pain d'épice'), Chef Maxime also pays tribute to this noble animal.

Canberra (AUSTRALIA)
Dessert: Lamington chocolate delight
Lamington cakes are an Australian national dish, named after Lamington, a former governor of Queensland (a province in Australia). The square dessert, covered in chocolate and coconut, has inspired Chef Collard to create a new, refined and state-of-the-art Belgian chocolate mousse dessert offering an explosion of tastes.

Serves 6

Goose liver Maxime's way // Budapest

Baked goose liver crumble,
beetroot medley,
turnip and turmeric chutney,
sauce with gingerbread spices

Crumble
50 g flour (1.8 oz) // 50 g (¼ cup) butter // 50 g (1.8 oz) ground almonds // 30 g (1.1 oz) sugar // 2 g (1 dr) paprika // salt and pepper
Mix together all the ingredients and spread in a layer approximately 2 cm (0.8 inch) deep on a baking sheet lined with greaseproof paper. Bake for about 12 minutes at 180 °C (356 °F).

Savoury tuiles
9 g (5 dr) flour // 3 g (1.7 dr) cornflour // 60 ml (2 fl oz) chicken stock // 20 ml (0.7 fl oz) olive oil // 20 ml (0.7 fl oz) water // 4 g (2.2 dr) melted butter
Mix all the ingredients. Heat a frying pan and pour in about 1 tablespoon of the batter. Tilt the pan to ensure that the batter spreads as thinly and evenly as possible. Cook for about 1 minute and a half. The tuile is ready when it stops crackling. Remove gently from the pan onto a plate using a thin spatula.

Turnip and turmeric chutney
2 turnips // 20 g (0.7 oz) honey // 50 ml (1.7 fl oz) white vinegar // 200 ml (6.8 fl oz) clear stock // turmeric // salt and pepper
Peel the turnips and blend. Heat the honey, vinegar and turmeric in a small saucepan. Add the turnips and the stock. Reduce until the liquid has evaporated. Season to taste.

Sauce with gingerbread spices
1 cinnamon stick // 4 star anise // 5 g (0.2 oz) green anise // black pepper // the zest of 1 orange // 50 g (1.8 oz) honey // 100 ml (3.4 fl oz) vinegar // 200 ml (6.8 fl oz) clear stock // soy sauce
Roast the spices in the oven (cinnamon, star anise, green anise, pepper and orange peel). Put in a pan with the honey and heat until golden brown. Deglaze with the vinegar and the stock. Reduce to a syrup. Season to taste with the soy sauce.

Beetroot medley
6 small beetroots // 1 Chioggia beetroot // 1 yellow beetroot // 2 tablespoons of honey // 100 ml (3.4 fl oz) vinegar // 300 ml (10 fl oz) water
Peel and cook each type of beetroot separately in a honey-vinegar-water mixture, reserving the cooking liquids. Put aside the small red beetroots, and using pastry-cutters cut different sizes of circles from the sliced yellow and Chioggia beetroot. Season very lightly with vinegar before serving. Reduce the red and yellow beetroot juices to obtain two vividly coloured sauces.

Parsley coulis
A bunch of parsley // salt and pepper
Blanch the parsley, blend and season.

Baked goose liver
6 slices goose liver, approximately 80 g (2.8 oz) each
Cook the goose liver slices in a hot frying pan without oil or butter, ensuring both sides are well coloured.

Assembly
Pour the three sauces (parsley coulis, yellow and red beetroot reductions) attractively onto the plate, and place the liver on top. Drizzle the spiced sauce over the liver and sprinkle the crumble on top. Decorate with the small red beetroot, the yellow and Chioggia beetroot slices, and the turnip chutney. Garnish with the tuiles and some yarrow (or another herb of your choice).

This exquisite dish deserves something special: a blond 'brut' beer following the original method: **Malheur Brut**. Beer guru Michael Jackson once described it as the new 'World Classic'. Strong but at the same time smooth as silk, aromatic with a beautiful bittersweet finish, it will complement the different gustative layers of this savoury dish.
www.malheur.be

MAXIME COLLARD

Budapest

Serves 6

Kudu of the Ardennes forests // Pretoria

Gingerbread ('pain d'épice') crusted fillet of Ardennes venison,
quince chutney with saffron and tonka bean,
Jerusalem artichoke, red cabbage cannelloni
huntsman's sauce

Gingerbread crust
50 g (1.8 oz) fine breadcrumbs // 50 g (1.8 oz) butter // 1 egg // 10 g (0.4 oz) gingerbread spices (cinnamon, green anise, star anise, coriander and cloves // 1 tablespoon mustard // salt and pepper
Mix together all the ingredients and season to taste. Spread the mixture between 2 sheets of baking paper, to a thickness of 2 mm (0.08 inch). Leave in the fridge until hardened. Cut to the same dimensions as the venison fillets.

Quince chutney
2 quinces // 50 g (1.8 oz) honey // 50 ml (1.7 fl oz) white vinegar // saffron // 2 tonka beans // salt
Peel and finely dice the quinces. Cook the quince with the honey, saffron, tonka beans and vinegar until you obtain a compote. Season.

Mashed Jerusalem artichoke and Jerusalem artichoke crisps
200 g (7 oz) Jerusalem artichokes
Peel and cook the Jerusalem artichokes in salted water. Mash and season to taste.
To make the Jerusalem artichoke crisps, cut thin slices and cook them in the fryer at 180 °C (356 °F).

Red cabbage cannelloni
1 onion // ½ red cabbage // a dash of white vinegar // 1 jonagold apple // 100 ml (3.4 fl oz) stock // salt and pepper // 1 daikon // 1 or 2 teaspoon honey
Chop the onion and sweat gently with some butter, then add the finely chopped red cabbage. Add the chopped apple and the mixture of honey, vinegar and stock. Slice the daikon in fine strips (approx 2 mm (0.08 inch)) with a mandoline. Put the cooked red cabbage mixture on the daikon slices and roll to form a cannelloni. Cut diagonally in half.

Daikon circle
1 daikon // 1 tablespoon honey // 1 tablespoon white vinegar // 1 teaspoon turmeric // salt and pepper
Finely slice the daikon and, cut out large circles using a pastry-cutter. Cook in a mixture of honey, vinegar, turmeric, salt and pepper.

Huntsman's sauce
1 kg (2.2 lbs) venison bones // 1 l (1 quart) red wine // 1 teaspoon juniper berry // 1 piece of dark chocolate // 1 tablespoon redcurrant jelly // salt and pepper // vegetables and herbs for the stock (onions, carrots, celery, thyme, bay leaves, etc.)
Make a stock from the venison bones, red wine, vegetables and juniper berries.
Strain the broth once it is cooked. Reduce with a tablespoon of redcurrant jelly. Add the chocolate and season to taste. Bind the sauce using cornstarch if necessary.

Venison fillet
6 × 150 g (6 × 5.3 oz) venison fillet
Quickly brown the fillets on each side. Put the gingerbread crust on top of the fillets and place in the oven for 3 to 4 minutes at 180 °C (356 °F).

Assembly
Garnish with Brussels sprout leaves (blanched for one minute in boiling water and then tossed in butter), dried ground cabbage leaf and fried celery leaves. Serve with the sauce.

A solid Trappist beer is the perfect match for game. Try **aged Orval** (over six months old). It is a multi-faceted amber beer with the specific taste of Orval yeast, bitter, hoppy, fruity and spicy tones and somewhat sour in taste.
www.orval.be

Pretoria

Serves 6

Lamington chocolate delight // Canberra

Chocolate praline mousse, hazelnut biscuit, speculoos and coffee ice cream

Lotus speculoos ice cream
300 ml (10.1 fl oz) milk // 200 ml (6.8 fl oz) whipping cream (35% fat) // 3 egg yolks // 80 g (¼ cup) sugar // 40 g (1.4 oz) crushed Lotus speculoos biscuits

Whisk the egg yolks and sugar until thick and creamy. Heat the milk and cream together, then add the eggs and sugar and stir over a gentle heat until the mixture coats the back of the wooden spoon. Allow to cool before pouring into an ice cream maker with the ground speculoos. When the ice cream is ready put into silicone quenelle moulds and store in the freezer.

Coffee ice cream
300 ml (10.1 fl oz) milk // 200 ml (6.8 fl oz) whipping cream (35% fat) // 3 egg yolks // 80 g (¼ cup) sugar // 20 ml (0.7 fl oz) coffee concentrate

Prepare in the same way as the speculoos ice cream, using coffee concentrate instead of the ground speculoos.

Chocolate praline mousse
250 g (8.8 oz) 70% dark chocolate // 50 g (1.8 oz) milk chocolate // 50 g (1.8 oz) praline // 20 g (1.5 el) butter // 2 egg yolks // 10 g (0.35 oz) sugar // 1 egg white // 1 sheet of gelatine // 80 ml (2.7 fl oz) whipping cream

Melt the chocolate with the praline and butter in a bain-marie. Whip the egg whites until they hold peaks. Whisk the egg yolks and sugar until thick and creamy, and gently add the melted chocolate, followed by the egg whites and the gelatine (which has been softened in cold water). Whip the cream to soft peaks and add to the mousse. Divide the mixture between square silicone moulds and moulds in the shape of quenelles and balls. Put in the fridge. When set, spray the balls and quenelles using metallic bronze and copper food colour sprays. Keep cool.

Hazelnut biscuit
40 g (⅓ cup) flour // 40 g (¼ cup) ground hazelnuts// 40 g (1.4 oz) sugar // 80 g (2.8 oz) egg white // 65 g (2.3 oz) sugar // 55 g (1.9 oz) egg yolk // 105 g (3.7 oz) butter, melted

Whisk the egg whites and sugar to form stiff peaks. Add the egg yolks. Stir in the flour, ground hazelnuts and sugar. Finally, add the melted butter. Thickly spread the mixture onto a baking sheet to a height of approximately 2 cm (0.8 inch). Bake for about 10 minutes at 180 °C (356 °F). When cool, cut into small circles using a pastry cutter.

Gingerbread tuile
100 g (0.4 cup) melted butter // 200 g (1 cup) sugar // 100 g (3.5 oz) flour // 50 ml (1.7 fl oz) water // 50 g (1.8 oz) egg white // 2 g (1 dr) gingerbread spices (cinnamon, ginger, clove, nutmeg, aniseed)

Mix all the ingredients together and spread a thin layer of dough onto a baking sheet lined with greaseproof paper. Bake for 10 minutes at 180 °C (356 °F). When cool, spray with metallic bronze food colour. Break into leaf-shaped pieces.

Assembly
Place the various chocolate mousse shapes on a plate. Garnish to taste with a line of crushed hazelnuts, the hazelnut biscuits and the leaf-shaped tuiles on each side. Add the ice cream quenelles to the plate just before serving.

If you're a chocolate lover, you're in for an extra treat. Enhance the delicious dessert with **Ardenne Stout**. Dark brown like chocolate, its taste also reminds of chocolate, a hint of coffee, a trace of cinnamon and roasted aromas with a bitter touch.

www.brasseriedebastogne.be

MAXIME COLLARD

Canberra

The heart of an avant-garde artist beats within Chef De Mangeleer as he stands behind the stove. With just a few strokes, amazing edible artefacts appear on your plate, as if by magic. But do not be mistaken; this cuisine may seem simple, but is far from it. That is how Michelin complimented him when awarding his third Michelin star. De Mangeleer is unique. He has mastered the art of creating exquisite flavour associations and accomplished menus based on refined and natural ingredients. He is continuously seeking fresh inspiration from home and abroad and is naturally attracted to the subtlety of Asian cuisine which is always striving to find the essence.
www.gertdemangeleer.com

Chef De Mangeleer fulfills all our expectations when dedicating his menu to the **Embassies of Belgium** in **Beijing** (China), **Tokyo** (Japan) and **London** (United Kingdom).

Gert De Mangeleer

Always striving for purity, to find the essence

Beijing (CHINA)

Starter: Dim sum stars

Chinese cuisine wouldn't be the same without dim sum. For centuries, meat, fish, vegetables and even sweets have been wrapped in dough and then steamed or deep-fried. Chef De Mangeleer makes his own version by wrapping his filling of Belgian langoustine in pumpkin from his own garden before laying it on cushions saturated with exotic fruits.

Tokyo (JAPAN)

Main dish: North Sea sushi

Japanese sushi are the latest trend and come in all sorts of shapes and sizes. Nigiri sushi is the best known and the noblest of all. An artistically moulded ball of rice with a piece of raw fish attached to it. This concept has inspired Chef De Mangeleer to create something new – a spinach roll with red pepper and pork instead of the rice and the raw Japanese fish is replaced by fried squid from the North Sea.

London (UNITED KINGDOM)

Dessert: From Flanders fields

For the British, Flanders Fields will always bring to mind the poppies that flourish at the sites of the First World War and have become a symbol of remembrance for all who have been destroyed by war. Based on flowers and herbs from these Flemish fields as well as Belgian speculoos (a type of spiced biscuit), Chef De Mangeleer has created a fairytale tartlet.

Serves 6 or more

Dim sum stars   // Beijing

Dim sum of butternut squash with Zeebrugge langoustine, spices and passion fruit

Marinated shallot
4 shallots // 200 ml (6.8 fl oz) soy sauce // 100 ml (3.4 fl oz) sherry vinegar

Finely chop the shallots. Mix with the soy sauce and sherry vinegar and heat to 80 °C (175 °F). Allow to cool in the refrigerator.

Langoustine oil
200 g (7 oz) langoustine heads // 200 g (7 oz) grape seed oil

Cook the langoustine heads in a little oil in a frying pan until they colour. Add the remaining oil and allow to infuse for 2 hours on a low heat. Strain through a fine sieve.

Mixture of herbs and spices
Mix 5 g (0.2 oz) black cardamom, 5 g (0.2 oz) tonka bean, 5 g (0.2 oz) wattle seeds and 5 g (0.2 oz) ground cocoa nibs.

Passion fruit and mango cream
375 g 13.2 oz) mango purée // 200 g (7 oz) passion fruit purée // 50 g (¼ cup) sugar // 6 g (0.2 oz) agar-agar

Mix the passion fruit and mango purées with the sugar and agar-agar. Bring to the boil and allow to boil for 10 seconds. Pour into a deep dish and allow to set in the refrigerator. When the purée is completely cold, process it in the blender. Strain through a fine sieve before using it to fill a piping bag.

Vanilla oil
For one bottle of vanilla oil, you will need ½ l (18 fl oz) of grape seed oil and one vanilla pod. Make sure you extract the seeds. Leave everything in a warm place to infuse for 4 hours. Strain, making sure to push all the seeds through the sieve for maximum vanilla flavour.

Langoustine gravy
3 kg (6.6 lbs) langoustine heads // 250 g (8.8 oz) onions // 3 garlic cloves // ½ head of celery // 250 g (8.8 oz) carrots // 20 g (0.7 oz) salt // 750 ml (1.3 pint) white wine // 2 l (3 ½ pint) water // 200 g (7 oz) egg white // soured cream

Cook the langoustine heads in hot oil until they colour. Add the vegetables and salt and cover with the water and wine. Bring to the boil and allow to simmer for about 25 minutes. Strain and then reduce gently until you have a concentrated stock. Clarify the stock with the egg white. Finish with the soured cream (using a ratio of 2 to 1, ie ½ l (17 fl oz) of soured cream for 1 l (35 fl oz) of stock).

Dim sum
6 large langoustines (size 6/8) // 1 butternut squash // 1 passion fruit

Clean the langoustines and remove the intestinal tract. Finely chop the langoustines. Mix about 80 g (2.8 oz) of the langoustine tartare with 15 g (0.5 oz) of marinated shallot, 1 g (0.6 dr) of salt and 9 g (5 dr) of langoustine oil. Thinly slice the butternut squash and cut out 7 cm (2.8 inch) circles. Blanch the slices for 5 seconds in boiling water. Immediately refresh in iced water and pat dry. Place 6 passion fruit seeds on each slice of butternut squash and put 10 g (0.35 oz) of the langoustine tartare on top. Fold the dim sums into the desired shape.

Assembly
Slightly moisten the dim sum with water and season them gently with the spice mixture. Pipe 2 rosettes of passion fruit-mango cream onto each plate. Place a seasoned dumpling on top of each rosette, before finishing with the vanilla oil. Serve with the hot, foamy langoustine gravy.

This elegant dish resonates with a well-balanced hoppy beer. L'Arogante claims to be the most Belgian and the 'hoppiest', quite audacious as its name suggests... which in fact is a merger of the names of two beautiful Belgian cities: La Roche-en-Ardenne and Ghent (Gand in French). This blonde beer offers a pleasant bitter aftertaste, citrusy hop aromas and a malty backbone that strengthens the full-bodied side of the butternut and langoustine.

www.larogante.be

Peking

Serves 6

North Sea Sushi   // Tokyo

Nigiri style sushi with squid, chorizo, pork leg and red pepper sauce

Red pepper sauce
100 g (3.5 oz) onion // 8 g (0.3 oz) garlic // 140 g (4.9 oz) leeks // 160 g (5.6 oz) red peppers // 800 g (1.7 lbs) tomatoes // 500 ml (18 fl oz) fish stock // 0.5 g (0.3 dr) smoked paprika // 100 g (3.5 oz) butter // 20 g (0.7 oz) tomato paste // 2.5 g (1.4 dr) salt

Chop the onion, garlic and leeks, and cook gently in some butter. Peel the pepper and remove its seeds. Chop the pepper and tomatoes and add to the pan. Allow to cook on a low heat. Add the fish stock and allow to simmer for 30 minutes. Process in a blender, then pass through a fine sieve. To finish, add the paprika, the remaining butter and the tomato paste and season with salt. Blend again until the sauce is completely smooth.

Spinach roll
1 onion // 45 g (1.6 oz) chorizo // 15 g (½ oz) sun-dried peppers // 75 g (2.6 oz) pork leg, cooked in stock and boned // 3 cloves of garlic // 3 g (1.7 dr) fresh peppercorns // sea salt // 500 g (17.6 oz) large spinach leaves // 1 courgette // 100 g (3.5 oz) sun-dried tomatoes

Finely chop the onion, and cut the chorizo, the sun-dried peppers and the pork leg into small cubes (about 1 mm (0.04 inch)). Sweat the onion and chorizo in some butter. Add the garlic, pork, and sun dried peppers, season with the fresh peppercorns and salt and cook for a few minutes. Set aside.

Blanch the spinach leaves in boiling water for 3 seconds. Immediately refresh in iced water and pat dry. Cut the cooked spinach leaves into 14 cm (5 ½ inch) squares. Divide the filling into portions of about 25 g (0.9 oz) and put one portion on each spinach sheet. Roll tightly into cannelloni. Place a thin slice of courgette and a slice of sun-dried tomato on top. Keep warm in the oven.

Nigiri style squid
2 large fresh, cleaned squids (approx 1 kg (2.2 lbs) each) // Japanese pepper // smoked paprika // sea salt

Cut the squid into 7.5 cm (3 inch) squares, and score their insides with a pattern of tiny (2 mm (0.08 inch)) squares. Heat the squid very briefly in a little oil until it starts to curl. Place a piece of squid on each spinach roll. Neatly trim the sides so that they are completely even. Sprinkle with the Japanese pepper, smoked paprika and sea salt. Serve with the warm, foamed sweet pepper sauce.

The 'saison' originates from the farms of Wallonia. It was given to drink to the 'saisoniers' working on the fields. The copper blond **Saison Dupont**, a complex and particular aromatic beer, is the most iconic of Belgium's saisons. Its earthy tones pick up on the meat and red pepper used in this recipe while it's spicy freshness lifts the umami and salty notes off the palate, leaving a dry finish with a touch of bitterness.

www.brasserie-dupont.com

7 TOP CHEFS CREATE A MENU FOR 21 EMBASSIES OF BELGIUM

Tokyo

Serves 12 or more

From Flanders fields

// London

Floral tartlet with Belgian speculoos and fromage frais cream

Lotus speculoos base

625 g (22 oz) Lotus speculoos biscuits, crumbled // 200 g (1 ²/₃ cup) flour // 100 g (3.5 oz) butter

Knead the crushed speculoos with the butter and flour until they form a ball. Roll out very thinly and cut into 7 cm (2.8 inch) rounds. Bake at 160 °C (320 °F) for 15 minutes. Allow to cool.

Fromage frais cream

250 g (8.8 oz) fromage frais // 80 g (2.8 oz) soured cream // 80 g (2.8 oz) cream // 50 g (1.8 oz) egg // 30 g (1 oz) egg yolk // 100 g (½ cup) sugar // 5 g (0.2 oz) leaf gelatine

Mix the fromage frais, the soured cream and the cream in a saucepan and heat until it comes to the boil. Whisk together the egg yolk, egg and sugar, beat well and add this mixture to the fromage frais. Heat to 85 °C (185 °F) before adding the gelatine, previously soaked in cold water. Process the mixture in a blender, and strain through a fine sieve. Allow it to firm up in the fridge before using it to fill a piping bag.

Iced rose pearls

500 g (1.1 lbs) yoghurt // 500 g (1.1 lbs) rose tea (1 l (1 quart) water, 500 g (2 ½ cup) sugar, 250 g (8.8 oz) fresh rose petals) // 5 g (0.2 oz) gelatine

Infuse the sugar and rose petals for 15 minutes in boiling water to make the tea. Strain the tea and mix with the yogurt and the soaked gelatine. Fill spherical moulds (smaller than a marble) with the mixture and freeze until firm.

Assembly

Fresh green herbs such as basil, different varieties of mint, marigold, fennel, lemon verbena, candyleaf, clover … // Assorted edible flowers such as marigold, hot lips, begonia, sage, fennel, mint … // 1 carton blueberries

Pipe 6 rosettes of the fromage frais cream onto each speculoos base. Place a blueberry next to each rosette. Decorate with the fresh herbs and flowers and, just before serving, add 3 iced pearls onto each tartlet.

This elegant dessert topped with fresh flowers and herbs requires a fresh-tasting and mild beer. **Cuvée des trolls**, named after Tolkien's trilogy, is a blonde unfiltered brew which is full in the mouth and has plenty of fruity citrus aromas. That's thanks to the addition of dried orange zest to this beer's ingredient's list. With its light bitter finish, it enhances the freshness of the dessert without being dominant.
www.dubuisson.com

London

This top chef from Antwerp could just as easily have been a brilliant architect or designer. His natural flair for harmony, proportion and beauty is not only expressed in each of his dishes, it also radiates from the magnificent decor of his acclaimed restaurant, **De Pastorale**. In this exquisitely refurbished presbytery, Chef Bart De Pooter's own culinary passion blends seamlessly with the creative expression of the many famous Belgian artists whose work catches your eye at every turn, and further nourishes you as you dine. De Pooter finds inspiration in the impressions and experiences that stem from his travels in every corner of the world. – www.depastorale.be

Chef De Pooter has drawn inspiration for his menu from the **Embassies of Belgium in Madrid** (Spain) and **Tunis** (Tunisia) and **the Consulate General of Belgium in Istanbul** (Turkey).

Bart De Pooter

An interaction between art and gastronomy

Madrid (SPAIN)

Starter: Bacon and cabbage flamenco
As in Belgium, pork in its many guises – including sausages, ham, charcuterie – is particularly valued in Spain. De Pooter here proves that a dish based on bacon can also be very refined. Combined with cabbage, another staple of Belgian cuisine, it becomes a swirling dance of flavours.

Istanbul (TURKEY)

Main dish: When West meets East
The blue crab is highly prized by tourists along the Turkish Riviera. Chef De Pooter here puts its cousin, the Belgian North Sea crab, to the fore while his Turkish spices evoke the famous and colourful Spice Bazaar of Istanbul.

Tunis (TUNISIA)

Dessert: A sweet dessert from the medina
Tunisians have a very sweet tooth, which has inspired Chef De Pooter to create a dessert that combines the African sweet potato with Belgian ice cream and an orange topping straight out of the medina of Tunis.

Serves 10

Bacon and cabbage flamenco // Madrid

Bacon, sauerkraut, cabbage

Bacon
1 kg (2.2 lbs) lightly salted bacon
Cook the bacon for 48 hours at 62 °C (144 °F) sous-vide. Divide into 10 pieces and fry until golden brown.

Sauerkraut gravy
50 g (1.8 oz) shallot // 200 g (7 oz) sauerkraut // 70 g (2.5 oz) olive oil //700 ml (1 ½ pint) chicken stock // 10 sage leaves // 2 cloves of garlic // 10 white peppercorns // 2 cardamom pods // 1 star anise // 1 g (15 gr) smoked paprikapowder // lemon
Gently cook the finely chopped shallot with the sauerkraut in some olive oil. Add the stock, followed by the crushed garlic and the spices (in a metal tea infuser) and let everything cook for about 20 minutes. Mix and pass through a fine sieve. Season with salt and lemon juice.

White cabbage
1 white cabbage // goose fat // fleur de sel // pepper
Bake the white cabbage whole at 180 °C (356 °F) for 3 hours. Remove the blackened outer leaves and cut into wedges. Fry the cabbage wedges in goose fat until golden. Season with a pinch of fleur de sel and freshly ground pepper.

Assembly
Serve the bacon and cabbage wedges garnished with small green cabbage leaves, which have been wilted in a pan. Scatter with fresh garden herbs (such as marjoram and flat parsley) and smoked paprikapowder. Serve with the sauerkraut gravy.

This seemingly straightforward dish can be paired with a fresh and lively beer: **Corsendonk Agnus**. The very clean palate balances the acidic, salty and 'earthy' components of this dish. This golden-yellow clear abbey tripel begins with a dry, lightly citric fruitiness and finishes with a distinctive and delicate, perfumey, hop character.
www.reclameturnhout.be

7 TOP CHEFS CREATE A MENU FOR 21 EMBASSIES OF BELGIUM

BART DE POOTER

Madrid

75

Serves 10

When West meets East

// Istanbul

North Sea crab, butternut squash, Turkish spices

Court-bouillon
3 carrots // 1 leek // ¼ head celery // 1 onion // 100 g (3.5 oz) fresh ginger // 50 g (1.8 oz) turmeric root // 40 g (1.40 oz) salt // 4 l (0.9 gallon) water

Court bouillon is essential for cooking the crab. Finely chop the carrots, leek, celery, onion, ginger and turmeric root. Add the water and salt and bring to a boil. Allow to simmer for half an hour with the lid of the pan slightly tilted. Strain the liquid through a fine sieve.

Crab salad
3 kg (6.6 lbs) crab legs // 80 g (2.8 oz) egg yolk // 300 g (10.5 oz) olive oil // 2 g (1.1 dr) turmeric // 30 g (1 oz) ginger juice // 1 g (15 gr) fenugreek // 30 g (1.06 oz) lime juice // 50 g (1.8 oz) crab court-bouillon // 20 g (0.7 oz) ginger syrup

Boil the crab legs for 5 minutes in the court-bouillon. Remove the crab meat from the legs.
Lightly whisk the egg yolk at room temperature, before adding the olive oil in a steady steam and continuing to whisk to a mayonnaise. Add the spices followed by the bouillon and the lime juice. Mix the mayonnaise with the crab.

Roasted butternut squash
1 butternut squash // 100 g (3.5 oz) finely chopped fresh ginger // 50 g (1.8 oz) turmeric // olive oil

Halve the pumpkin lengthwise. Rub the cut side with some oil, the ginger, turmeric and a pinch of salt. Leave in the oven for 2 hours at 160 °C (320 °F).

Crab gravy
75 g (2.6 oz) olive oil // 350 g (12.3 oz) brown crab meat // 30 g (1 oz) shallots // 40 g (1.4 oz) celery // 60 g (2 oz) carrot // 50 g (1.8 oz) ginger root // 5 g (0.2 oz) turmeric root // 2 l (3 ½ pint) chicken stock // 2 g (1 dr) turmeric // 30 g (1 oz) ginger juice // 50 g (1.8 oz) sushi vinegar

Cut the vegetables and sweat in some olive oil. Add the crab meat. Moisten regularly with the chicken stock and allow to cook for 20 minutes. Strain through a fine sieve. Cook the strained liquid until reduced to ⅓ of the initial volume. Season with turmeric, ginger juice and sushi vinegar. If desired, add a few pieces of the roasted squash to thicken the gravy.

Assembly
Pour a spoonful of crab gravy onto the plate. Make a row of evenly-sliced butternut squash. Arrange the crab salad on top. Decorate with a few leaves of green herbs, pomegranate seeds and black sesame seeds.

A light and fresh white beer is the perfect liaison between West and East, land and sea. Impossible to resist the charms of **Blanche de Namur**. Notes of coriander and dried orange peel offer a pure, slightly spicy and citrusy aroma, nicely enhancing the delicate taste of the crab. The smooth mouthfeel evokes the dish's more earthy components. www.bocq.be

Istanbul

Serves 10

A sweet dessert from the medina // Tunis

Sweet potato, ice cream, orange, milk foam

Ice cream
2 l (3 ½ pint) semi-skimmed milk // 150 g (5.3 oz) milk powder // 4 sheets of gelatine // 200 g (7 oz) cream // 50 g (1.8 oz) butter
Bring the milk to the boil, then add the milk powder, the cream and the butter whilst stirring continuously. Allow to cool and add the soaked gelatine when mixture reaches 40 °C (104 °F). Allow to cool completely in the fridge, before freezing in an ice-cream maker.

Sweet potato cubes
5 sweet potatoes
Bake the sweet potatoes in the oven at 180 °C (356 °F) for 40 minutes. Peel and roughly cut into cubes. They can be served cold or lukewarm.

Confit oranges
200 g (7 oz) sugar // 100 ml (3.4 fl oz) water // 3 oranges
Rinse and clean the oranges before cutting into 5 mm (0.2 inch) slices. Put the slices in the sugar syrup and bring to a boil. Lower the temperature and allow the slices to cook gently for 1 hour at 80 °C (176 °F). Allow to cool in the sugar syrup. Remove from the syrup and place on a cake rack. Leave to rest for at least 12 hours. Repeat this procedure 3 times with 50 ml (1.7 fl oz) of water being added each time.

Fresh orange segments
Remove the peel and pith from 5 oranges and carefully cut the segments away from the membrane. Allow 5 segments per person.

Assembly
Ghoa cress // orange and lime zests // 2 dl (6.8 fl oz) milk // vanilla sugar
Put a scoop of ice cream onto a plate and place the sweet potato cubes on top. Finish with pieces of confit orange, orange segments and some milk foam, which is made just before serving by heating the milk (to 55 °C (131 °F)) with a little vanilla sugar and then whisking with an electric milk frother. Garnish with the freshly grated lime and orange zests, and the Ghoa cress.

The Belgian-style Belgian Quadrupel is a warming and mostly sweet beer, high in alcohol and bold in flavour. **Sint Bernardus Abt 12**, internationally acclaimed, is a beautiful example of this type of beer. It has a full-bodied taste and a long bittersweet finish with a hoppy bite, which goes very well with a sweet and fruity dessert.
www.sintbernardus.be

7 TOP CHEFS CREATE A MENU FOR 21 EMBASSIES OF BELGIUM

Tunis

For two decades, chef Sang Hoon Degeimbre has been outdoing himself while developing a resolutely innovative style of cooking. In his restaurant, **L'Air du Temps**, he makes the most of the best the land has to offer him. In so doing, he demonstrates a solemn respect for nature: his kitchen is in tune with the seasons, there is zero waste, and he tries to find cooking methods requiring less energy and minimal water consumption. Furthermore, in the gardens surrounding his restaurant he produces 90% of the vegetables, herbs and fruits needed for his dishes.
As founder of Génération W, a group of Walloon chefs and local food producers, he makes every effort to give prominence to the Walloon terroir on his menu. His creativity, passion and powerful dishes have made Sang Hoon Degeimbre a favoured ambassador of Belgian haute cuisine around the world. – **www.airdutemps.be**

Passion for the land and creativity in the air

Especially for the **Belgian Embassies in Paris** (France), **Amman** (Jordan) and **New Delhi** (India), Chef Degeimbre has created three particularly subtle dishes:

Sang Hoon Degeimbre

Paris (FRANCE)
Starter: A Brussels waffle in Paris
The Brussels waffle, so light and so delicious when topped with whipped cream, strawberries or chocolate, is the starting point. By adding Paris mushrooms, the most popular mushroom in the world, the two culinary capitals come together in a feast for your eyes and taste buds.

Amman (JORDAN)
Main dish: Wadi Rum
Chef Degeimbre takes you on a voyage through the legendary desert of Wadi Rum. The adventure starts with the preparation of this dish. The desert winds force the reddish dunes of this lunar landscape to gradually reveal their secrets. A surprising Belgian blue, Jordanian style, comes to the surface.

New Delhi (INDIA)
Dessert: Millefeuille namaste
Chef Degeimbre designed this millefeuille to express his admiration for the refinement of Indian civilization and the multiple layers of its cuisine: a rich diversity of ingredients, scents, colours and flavours. The result is an amazing combination of potato, white chocolate, cardamom and cuberdon (a cone-shaped Belgian candy)

Serves 8

A Brussels waffle in Paris

// Paris

Brussels waffle, foie gras, Paris mushrooms, lemon gel

Brussels waffle
18 ml (0.6 fl oz) sparkling water // 21 ml (0.7 fl oz) whole milk // 3 g (1.7 dr) instant yeast // 5 g (2.8 dr) vanilla sugar // 2 eggs // 5 g (2.8 dr) sugar // 4 g (2.2 dr) salt // 27 g (1 oz) sifted flour // 90 g (3.2 oz) butter

Separate the eggs. Mix together the yolks, sugar, salt and flour. In another bowl mix the butter, milk, yeast and vanilla. Heat to 60 °C (140 °F) until the butter melts. Pour both mixtures together and add the sparkling water. Beat the egg whites until they are stiff, and gently add to the batter. Allow to rest for 45 minutes. Cook in a waffle iron suitable for Brussels waffles (type B 3 × 5) for 4 minutes on thermostat 5. Turn the waffle iron immediately after pouring the batter. Set aside. Cut the cooked waffle into 4 small squares of waffle.

Foie gras
1 slice of fresh foie gras // salt and pepper

Cut the foie gras into pieces the size of the waffle squares. Finely slice these pieces and season.

Paris mushrooms
A box of fresh Paris mushrooms // salt // 2 packets of dried yeast

Finely slice half of the mushrooms and season with salt. Slice the other half into circles with the help of a cutter, and sprinkle with baked oven yeast crumbs.

Lemon gel
10 ml (0.35 fl oz) lemon juice // 50 ml (1.7 fl oz) water // 40 g (1.4 oz) sugar // 2 g (1.1 dr) agar-agar

Mix all ingredients together until completely dissolved. Bring to the boil and remove immediately from the heat. Stir vigorously and allow to cool. Blend with a hand blender in a tall receptacle until you have a gel.

Assembly
Put some lemon gel in the cavities of the waffle. Place the slices of foie gras on the waffle while seasoning each layer with salt and pepper. Then attach the mushrooms onto the foie gras using the lemon gel. Garnish with the sprinkled mushroom rounds and decorate the plate with lemon gel dots.

Caulier 28 saison with its earthy, spiced and citrusy aromas, completes the link between Brussels and Paris. Saisons were originally seasonal beers, brewed on the farms in Wallonia. The pronounced saison yeast aroma goes very well with the mushrooms. This crisp and light-bodied beer also gives a fresh note to the foie gras and repeats the perfume of the lemon gel.
www.caulier.be

7 TOP CHEFS CREATE A MENU FOR 21 EMBASSIES OF BELGIUM

Paris

Serves 8

Wadi Rum

// Amman

Beef, carrots, freekah risotto

Beef
500 g (1.1 lbs) entrecote (5 cm (2 inch) thick) // salt and pepper // grape seed oil

Allow the meat to reach room temperature before rubbing its surface with salt. Heat a little of the oil in a frying pan and, when hot, quickly sear each side for 30 seconds, repeating 4 times for each side. Cover the meat and allow to rest for 40 minutes in an oven at 80 °C (176 °F).

Carrot sand
30 g (1 oz) carrots // 30 g (1 oz) purple carrots // 30 g (1 oz) fermented carrots // 30 g (1 oz) fermented white carrots // 30 g (1 oz) sumac

To make the fermented carrots yourself, carefully wash the required amount of carrots. Prepare a brine for each type using 30 g (1 oz) of sea salt and a litre (1 quart) of water. Put the carrots into two jars that can be hermetically sealed and fill with brine to 1 cm (0.4 inch) below the rim. Seal the jars, and store in a cupboard at room temperature, with a plate underneath in case of any slight overflow. After a week, put the jars in the fridge (15 to 20 °C (59 to 68 °F)), and the fermented carrots will be ready to use in 3 weeks.

Peel the fresh carrots and finely grate each variety separately using a citrus zester. Thinly slice about twenty carrot rounds to use as a garnish. Dehydrate the grated carrots and slices by spreading them on a baking sheet and leaving in a 65-70 °C (150 to 158 °F) oven for about 1 ½ hours. In a food processor separately reduce each colour of grated and fermented carrots to sand. Combine the two different colours, along with some sumac, to replicate the reddish colour of the Wadi Rum desert.

Freekah risotto
60 g (2.1 oz) shallots // 100 g (3.5 oz) freekah // 200 ml (6.8 fl oz) white wine // 1 tablespoon olive oil // 300 ml (10 fl oz) chicken stock // knob of butter

Put the chopped shallots and the white wine in a pan and allow to cook until all the liquid has evaporated. Then add the olive oil and the freekah. When the wheat is translucent, gradually add the chicken stock. Stir occasionally until the liquid is absorbed. Finish it off with a knob of butter.

Carrot purée
100 g (3.5 oz) carrot // 20 g (0.7 oz) butter

Steam the carrots with the butter. Blend to a purée in a food processor.

Red wine sauce
60 g (2.1 oz) shallots // 50 ml (1.7 fl oz) port // 200 ml (6.8 fl oz) red wine // 500 ml (½ quart) veal stock // ½ teaspoon liquorice // 50 g (1.8 oz) butter // salt and pepper

Cook the chopped shallots, the red wine and the port until all the liquid has evaporated. Then add the veal stock and the liquorice. Reduce by two thirds, season and whisk in knobs of butter.

Alternative non-alcoholic sauce
60 g (2.1 oz) shallots // 30 ml (1 fl oz) balsamic vinegar // 200 ml (6.8 fl oz) verjus // 500 ml (1 pint) veal stock // 1 teaspoon of sugar // 50 g (1.8 oz) butter // salt and pepper

Cook the chopped shallot, verjus and balsamic vinegar until the liquid has completely evaporated. Add the veal stock and the sugar. Reduce by two thirds, season and whisk in the knobs of butter.

Assembly
Place the risotto in the centre of the plate. Make a small mound of carrot sand. Cut the beef into individual servings, then divide each serving into two pieces, and place on the carrot sand. Generously decorate with dots of carrot purée, and garnish with the carrot chips.

This exotic dish will be further enhanced by a traditional and authentic old style Belgium beer. **Bertinchamps triple** is a smooth, slightly amber and cloudy beer. Because of its softness with an invigorating bitterness in the aftertaste and discreet hints of caramel, it will be the perfect support for the seasoning of this dish.
www.bertinchamps.be

7 TOP CHEFS CREATE A MENU FOR 21 EMBASSIES OF BELGIUM

Amman

Serves 8

Millefeuille Namaste // New Delhi

Potato wafers, white chocolate cream with cardamom, cuberdon meringue

Potato wafer
300 g (10.6 oz) potatoes // 60 g (2 oz) sugar // 60 ml (2 fl oz) milk

Cook the peeled potatoes, drain and mash. Add the milk and sugar and blend everything in the food processor until you have a smooth dough. Allow to rest for an hour, then spread onto a silicone cooking mat and use a silicone stencil to make 8 cm × 3 cm (3.1 inch × 1.2 inch) rectangles. Bake at 130 °C (266 °F) for 10-15 minutes. Gently detach the wafers and set aside in a dry place.

Custard
75 ml (2.5 fl oz) milk // 75 ml (2.5 fl oz) whipping cream // 50 g (1.8 oz) egg yolk // 25 g (0.9 oz) sugar // 10 g (0.35 oz) white cardamom // 2 g (1.1 dr) gelatine

Heat the milk and cream together, add the cardamom and set aside to infuse for 2 hours. Blend the cooled mixture in a food processor, before straining. Beat the egg yolks with the sugar until pale and creamy, then add the strained cream. Cook the mixture at 83 °C (180 °F) until it coats the back of a spoon. Strain through a fine sieve. Dissolve the gelatine (previously soaked in cold water) in 150 ml (5.3 oz) of the liquid, combine with the remaining mixture and put in the fridge.

White chocolate cream with cardamom
225 g (8 oz) white chocolate // 250 g (8.8 oz) very cold whipping cream // 150 ml (5 fl oz) custard // cardamom

Melt the white chocolate in a bain-marie at a low temperature. Whip the cream. When the white chocolate reaches 40 °C (104 °F), add the custard and mix with a spatula until emulsified. Slowly add the whipped cream. Put in the fridge to set.

Cuberdon meringue
40 ml (1.4 fl oz) water // 30 g (1 oz) cuberdons (a Belgian candy) // 60 g (2 oz) sugar // 50 g (1.8 oz) egg white

Gently heat the water, cuberdons and sugar until everything is dissolved, then strain. Continue heating the mixture until it reaches 120 °C (248 °F). Meanwhile beat the egg whites, first at medium, and then at high, speed. Pour the cuberdon syrup over the egg whites while continuing to beat until the meringue has cooled. Pour into a flat piping bag.

Assembly
Take 5 potato wafers. Spread each layer with white chocolate mousse using a piping bag and finish with cuberdon meringue and some bursts of cuberdon (small frozen pieces, chopped at the last minute).

Gouden Carolus Triple, originally brewed for the Knights of the Golden Fleece in 1491, is world class. It received a gold award for 'World's Best Belgian-Style Tripel'. This pleasant golden-yellow beer, graceful and tender, with a clean and neat taste, will enchant you while you savour this delicate millefeuille. www.hetanker.be

SANG HOON DEGEIMBRE

New Delhi and Chennai

The much lauded **Sea Grill** is without a doubt one of the best fish restaurants in Belgium. Located in the Brussels Radisson Blu hotel, its contemporary cosmopolitan grandeur makes it a favourite mooring place for many a captain of industry. For the good-natured and enthusiastic Chef Mattagne, this multicultural work environment is a continuous source of inspiration. It's no wonder he has a finger in so many pies with a wealth of international projects bearing his name. Hospitable gastronomy is an art that Chef Mattagne exercises right down to his fingertips. Not only by serving eye-catching and tasty little miracles on the plate, but also through an exceptionally friendly and professional service at the table. – **www.seagrill.be**

A tribute to the sea in the heart of Brussels

Chef Mattagne's menu for the **Embassies of Belgium in Berlin** (Germany), **Abu Dhabi** (United Arab Emirates) and **Vienna** (Austria), sends us on a voyage of flavours, colours and smells.

Yves Mattagne

Berlin (GERMANY)

Starter: Berliner Art
'Leber Berliner Art', or Berlin Style Liver, is a traditional Berlin dish. This has inspired Chef Mattagne to refine the dish to a combination of liver and fish served on a bed of Belgian endive.

Abu Dhabi (UNITED ARAB EMIRATES)

Main dish: The Emir's Coucou de Malines
In honour of the luxurious Emirate of Abu Dhabi, Chef Mattagne has created an elegant dish, rich in Belgian specialties. He prepares the Coucou de Malines, a premium breed of Belgian chicken, in several ways and accompanies it with an airy béarnaise sauce studded with grey shrimps – one of the chef's signature dishes. And today you can still see these North Sea shrimps being fished on horseback in Oostduinkerke, the only place in the world where this tradition has been kept alive.

Vienna (AUSTRIA)

Dessert: Chocolate Waltz
The world famous Sachertorte from Vienna naturally leads Chef Mattagne to this sumptuous chocolate dessert, a swirling waltz of chocolate flavours and textures.

Serves 4

Berliner Art // Berlin

Scallops and foie gras, slow-cooked Belgian endives, truffle, gravy

Slow-cooked Belgian endives
12 endives // 30 g (1 oz) foie gras fat// clarified butter // salt and pepper // a pinch of sugar
Separate the endive leaves and blanch for 30 seconds in boiling salted water. Drain the leaves, then cook in clarified butter over a high heat until all the leaves are well coloured. Transfer to a saucepan and season with salt, pepper and a pinch of sugar. Add the foie gras fat and cover the contents of the saucepan with parchment paper. Allow to cook gently for 15 to 20 minutes over a low heat. Drain to remove excess fat.

Gravy
500 g (1.1 lbs) chicken legs // 25 g (0.9 oz) mushrooms // 30 g (1 oz) onions // 30 g (1 oz) leeks // 20 g (0.7 oz) celery // 15 g (0.5 oz) carrots // 1 clove garlic // ½ tomato // thyme and bay leaf // 200 ml (6.8 fl oz) chicken stock // 400 ml (13.5 fl oz) beef stock // butter
Cut the chicken legs into pieces and roast for 30 minutes at 180 °C (360 °F) until they are dry and golden. In a frying pan, sweat the vegetables with the thyme and bay leaf until soft and coloured, then add the chicken. Deglaze the roasting tin with all the stock and add to the frying pan. Cook for another 25 minutes. Strain through a fine sieve, and reduce to a thick sauce before whisking in the butter.

Scallops and foie gras
8 scallops // 4 slices fresh foie gras, approx 45 g (1.6 oz) each
Cook the scallops in oil and butter over a high heat. Then cook the slices of foie gras in the same way for about 30 seconds on each side. Season.

Potato spirals
Potatoes // oil
Using a spiralizer, make long strands of potato. Cover a tube with a diameter of 25 mm (1 inch) with greaseproof paper, then oil generously. Wrap the potato strands around the tube and fry at 130 °C (265 °F) until golden. Immediately remove the spiral from the tube and cut to the desired length.

Assembly
4 slices of raw mushrooms brushed with gold powder // the tips of 12 endive leaves // 8 g (4.5 dr) black truffle// 12 hazelnut halves // 4 nasturtium leaves
Put some slow-cooked endive on a plate and neatly place the scallops and foie gras on top. Garnish with golden mushroom slices, endive leaf tips, shavings of black truffle, hazelnuts and nasturtium leaves. Finish with a drizzle of sauce and the potato spirals.

A Trappist beer is very suitable for this complex and smooth starter. **Westmalle Dubbel** offers a rich pallet of flavours with caramel and malt aromas and even a hint of ripe banana, which go well with the endive confit. Its dry, bittersweet finish nicely balances the richness of the goose liver and scallops.
www.trapistwestmalle.be

Berlin

Serves 4

The emir's coucou de Malines   // Abu Dhabi

Coucou de Malines, béarnaise sauce with North Sea shrimps, Belgian cheese crumble, white asparagus, pomme bouchon

Coucou de Malines and its crispy skin
1 Coucou de Malines or other fattened young chicken // salt and pepper

Remove the breasts and thighs from the chicken, reserving the breast skin for the garnish. Spread a piece of clingfilm on the work surface. Season the breasts with salt and pepper and tightly roll each of them in clingfilm, tying a knot at each end so that they resemble two sausages. Debone the thighs, season and similarly roll in clingfilm.

Cook the breasts in a steam oven at 70 °C (160 °F) for 45 minutes (or for 20 minutes in a steamer), and the thighs at 75 °C (170 °F) for 2 hours (or for 35 minutes in a steamer). Allow to cool in the fridge and, once cooled, remove the plastic wrap and wrap them in the same way in oiled tinfoil. Keep in the fridge.

Spread the skin between 2 sheets of greaseproof paper and sandwich between 2 heavy baking trays. Bake at 170 °C (340 °F) for about 40 minutes. Immediately cut into squares and put on paper towels to absorb any surplus fat.

Béarnaise with grey shrimps
Gastrique of shallots

100 g (3.5 oz) chopped shallots // 250 ml (8.5 fl oz) red vinegar // 1 g (0.6 dr) crushed black pepper

Cook the chopped shallots, red vinegar and crushed black pepper together for 10 minutes. Strain through a fine sieve. Set aside the liquid.

Strong bisque
500 g (1.1 lbs) whole grey shrimps // olive oil // 50 g (1.8 oz) onions // 50 g (1.8 oz) leeks // 50 g (1.8 oz) celery // 50 g (1.8 oz) carrots // 2 cloves garlic // thyme, bay leaf // 250 g (8.8 oz) canned peeled tomatoes // 1 l water

Brown the shrimps in olive oil. Add the onions, leeks, celery, carrots, garlic cloves, thyme and bay leaf. Allow to cook gently before adding the peeled tomatoes. Add the water, bring to the boil and cook for 25 minutes. Strain through a fine sieve and reduce by ⅔.

Béarnaise mousseline
3 egg yolks // 1 teaspoon water // 1 teaspoon shallot vinegar // 250 g (8.8 oz) clarified butter // 120 ml (4 fl oz) cream // salt and pepper // 2 gas cartridges

Combine the egg yolks, water and shallot vinegar in a pan. Add the clarified butter little by little, while continuously whipping to a thick mousseline. Add the cream. Season and pour through a fine sieve. Put the mixture in a siphon and carbonate twice, using a fresh cartridge each time. Keep warm in a bain-marie at 50 °C (120 °F).

To finish the béarnaise
100 g (3.5 oz) peeled grey shrimp // 2 tablespoons reduced bisque // 2 teaspoons shallot gastrique // 1 teaspoon chopped estragon

Heat the bisque, add the shallot gastrique, put in a bowl and add the peeled shrimps (at room temperature). Cover the shrimps with béarnaise mousseline from the siphon and sprinkle with chopped estragon. Gently mix everything together.

Nazareth cheese crumble
100 g (3.5 oz) Nazareth cheese (or similar, eg Emmenthal) // 10 g (5.6 dr) flour

Grate the cheese and add the flour. Spread on a baking tray and bake at 170 °C (340 °F) for 15 to 20 minutes. Allow to cool and reduce to crumbs in a food processor.

Pommes bouchon
2 large potatoes // 2 cloves of garlic // butter // water // thyme and bay leaves

Cut cylinders of about 2 cm (0.8 inch) diameter from the potatoes. Arrange them upright in a pan, and add the garlic, thyme, bay leaves and water (to reach ¾ of the way up) before topping each piece with a knob of butter. Cook until the water is completely evaporated and the potatoes are nicely coloured. Keep warm.

We propose a sour ale, **Geuze Mariage Parfait** or 'perfect wedding'. This traditional old geuze is a blended, complex beer with surprising aromas of amongst others hay, vinegar, green apple, hop and citrus, which goes well with the rather acidic béarnaise sauce.

www.boon.be

Vegetables

4 spears white asparagus // 100 g (3.5 oz) mushrooms // 400 g (0.9 lbs) fresh spinach // garlic clove

Peel and cook the asparagus in salted boiling water. Sauté the mushrooms. Heat the spinach in a pan with butter and a clove of garlic.

Assembly

Heat some oil in a pan. Colour the chicken legs through the foil. Keep warm in a 65 °C (150 °F) oven and cut into slices before serving. Warm the chicken breasts in a steamer.

Heat the asparagus, the spinach and the mushrooms. Put the potatoes in the oven so that they are hot, not dry. Serve the spinach in a rectangular shape. Arrange as desired and serve the béarnaise separately.

Abu Dhabi

Serves 4

Chocolate waltz // Vienna

Creamy chocolate, pralines, vanilla mousse, cocoa gel, caramelized choco pops

Creamy chocolate
250 ml (8.5 fl oz) milk // 120 g (4.2 oz) cream // 120 g (4.2 oz) sugar // 100 g (3.5 oz) egg yolks // 120 g (4.2 oz) 64% dark chocolate

Bring the milk and cream to the boil. Beat the egg yolks and sugar together until pale and creamy, then add the boiling cream mixture. Stir well and cook until you have a custard. Remove from the heat and add the chocolate. Stir well and pour the creamy chocolate into soup plates (allowing about 80 g (2.8 oz) per person). Put in a cool place.

Praline of coffee granita
100 ml (3.4 fl oz) water // 100 g (3.5 oz) sugar // 150 ml (5 fl oz) strong coffee

Boil together the water and the sugar. Add the coffee and stir well. Allow to cool and place in a shallow container in the freezer. When crystals have formed, break up using a spoon to form the granita. Then shape the granita into small balls.

Praline of Amaretto mousse
100 ml (3.4 fl oz) milk // 100 ml (3.4 fl oz) cream // 60 g (2.1 oz) egg yolk // 60 g (2.1 oz) sugar // 2 sheets of gelatine // 125 g (4.4 oz) lightly whipped cream // 50 ml (1.7 fl oz) Amaretto // 8 chocolate shells // cocoa powder

Bring the milk and cream to the boil. Beat the egg yolks and the sugar together until pale and creamy, then add the boiling cream mixture. Stir well and cook until you have a custard. Add the gelatine, which has been soaked in water until soft. When the mixture has cooled, add the Amaretto and the lightly whipped cream. Fill the chocolate shells and sprinkle with cocoa.

Vanilla mousse
400 ml (13.5 fl oz) cream // 125 ml (4.2 fl oz) milk // 50 g (1.8 oz) sugar // 1 vanilla pod // 1 sheet gelatine (2 g (1.1 dr))

Bring the milk to the boil with the sugar and vanilla, and add the gelatine, previously soaked in cold water until soft. Strain through a sieve. Then add the lightly whipped cream and allow to cool. Put in a siphon with 2 gas cartridges.

Cocoa jelly
250 ml (8.5 fl oz) water // 90 g (3.2 oz) sugar // 40 g (1.4 oz) cocoa // 3 g (1. dr) of agar-agar // 2 sheets of gelatine

Bring the water, sugar and cocoa to the boil together. Add the agar-agar and the 2 sheets of gelatine, previously soaked in cold water. Return to the boil and then allow to cool completely. Process to obtain a smooth jelly. Put in a piping bag.

Cocoa crumble
50 g (1.8 oz) soft butter // 50 g (1.8 oz) sugar // 35 g (1.2 oz) ground almonds // 15 g (0.5 oz) ground hazelnuts // 50 g (1.8 oz) flour // a pinch of fleur de sel // 30 g (1 oz) cocoa powder

Mix all the ingredients. Spread on a silicone mat. Bake at 180 °C (360 °F) for 2 minutes. Allow to cool and process to a crumble.

Caramelized choco pops
Make a caramel with sugar, pour onto the choco pops and mix well. Pour on a silicone mat and let cool. Break into pieces.

Assembly
Sprinkle the crumble onto the creamy chocolate. Add the pralines and the choco pops. Make cocoa gel drops using a piping bag. Finish with the vanilla mousse and small decorations according to taste (mint, golden leaves, sweets).

Chocolate combined with fruit is a winning combination. If you like authentic cherry beer, go for **Oude Kriek 3 Fonteinen**, which is officially recognised and protected as a regional product. The cherry beer is made of young lambic beer in which sour cherries have ripened for 5 to 8 months. The result is a refreshing beer that carries besides fruity tones, some wood and vanilla aromas.

www.3fonteinen.be

Vienna

More than 25 years ago Pierre Résimont happened upon a small 17th century water mill along an idyllic river in the valleys of Namur, and it was love at first sight. So it was here he decided to set up his gourmet restaurant and it goes without saying that he called it **'L'Eau-Vive'** in honour of the water that rushes by. Since then it has become one of Belgium's leading restaurants. Chef Résimont maintains a perfect balance between continuous innovation and traditional dishes, and walks a fine line between taste and texture, so that every dish is masterful and exact. And what's more, the service is so impeccable that his guests can take a break from the everyday and step into this seventh heaven. – www.eau-vive.be

Chef Résimont 'goes with the flow' with his dishes for the **Embassies of Belgium in Rio de Janeiro** (Brazil), **Rome** (Italy) and **Bangkok** (Thailand).

Pierre Résimont

Running water, a source of inspiration and success

Rio de Janeiro (BRAZIL)

Starter: River trout for Rio

Clear, running water lets the river trout thrive. So it's not surprising that Chef Résimont has been inspired by this delicious local fish. The subtle link with Rio de Janeiro lies in the soy based sauce – Brazil is the world's largest soya bean producer.

Rome (ITALY)

Main dish: All … deer … lead to Rome

His restaurant being located within a stone's throw of the Ardennes forests, Chef Résimont's choice of a course based on game was to be expected. He gives the dish an Italian twist by adding an airy parmesan croquette.

Bangkok (THAILAND)

Dessert: The strawberries of Wépion meet Thailand

This complex dessert reveals the distinct and delicate flavours of Thai coconut and strawberries from Wépion, the small town near Namur renowned for the most prized specimens of this lovely fruit. This dessert is not only technically accomplished – Chef Résimont is an expert in the art of pâtisserie – but it's also a multisensory experience for the tastebuds.

Serves 6

River trout for Rio
// Rio de Janeiro

Brown trout fillet, soy emulsion, pork terrine

Brown trout fillet
2 brown trout fillets
Cook the trout fillets sous-vide for 15 minutes at 55 °C (130 °F), then slice them as shown in the picture.

Pickles
300 ml (1 1/3 cup) water // 200 ml (6.8 fl oz) white vinegar // 100 g (3.5 oz) sugar // 6 cauliflower florets in different colours // 100 g (3.5 oz) chanterelles
Bring the water, vinegar and sugar to the boil. Allow to cool, and pour over the cauliflower florets and the chanterelles. Store vacuum-packed for 3 to 4 days.

Parsley jelly round
100 g (3.5 oz) parsley // 100 ml (3.4 fl oz) water // 2 g (31 gr) agar-agar // 1 gelatine sheet
Bring the water to the boil, add the parsley and liquidise. Add the agar-agar and the gelatine sheet, previously soaked and drained. Pour into silicone moulds (11.5 cm (4.5 inch) round) and store in the fridge.

Onion garnish
1 onion
Slice the onion into rings using a mandoline and deep fry at 140 °C (285 °F) for 3 to 4 minutes.

Soy emulsion
40 g (1.4 oz) honey // 80 ml (2.7 fl oz) soy sauce // 16 g (0.5 oz) tomato ketchup // 2 g (31 gr) garlic // 32 g (1.1 oz) ginger // 250 ml (1 cup) oil // 1 tablespoon Xantan gum
Blend all the ingredients and strain through a fine conical sieve.

Pork terrine
225 g (8 oz) pig's trotters, bones removed // 15 g (0.5 oz) chopped shallot, fried until translucent // 225 g (8 oz) smoked bacon lardons fried // 10 g (6 dr) chopped parsley // 10 g (6 dr) chopped chives // 10 g (6 dr) chopped chervil // 12 g (7 dr) roasted pine nuts // 12 g (7 dr) roasted pistachios // 25 g (0.9 oz) minced poultry mixed with 150 g (5.3 oz) whipping cream // 1 egg // 75 g (2.6 oz) diced foie gras
Mix everything together and bake in terrine at 150 °C (300 °F) for 50 minutes. Allow to cool and cut into fine strips.

Assembly
Arrange the round of parsley jelly in the centre of the plate and place the slices of trout fillet and some pieces of pork terrine on top. Then pour a little soy emulsion onto the trout and garnish with the pickled vegetables.

A strong tripel pairs nicely with freshwater fish. The golden **Delirium Tremens** has some mild citrusy tones, herbal notes and spicy yeast flavours. You can even discern a hint of pepper which ignites the mouth. The aftertaste is strong, long-lasting and dry bitter. This beer has won several international awards.
www.delirium.be

PIERRE RÉSIMONT

Rio de Janeiro

Serves 4

All ... deer ... lead to Rome

// Rome

Saddle of venison, quince, Parmesan croquette

Venison
600 g (1 ¹/₃ lbs) saddle of venison // butter // salt and pepper

Debone the saddle of venison, keeping the bones for the stock. Season the venison fillets and colour them in hot butter, basting regularly. Allow to rest for 15 minutes.

Venison stock
2 kg (4 lbs 7 oz) of venison neck // 2 carrots // 1 onion // 2 shallots // 2 stalks of celery // 1 tablespoon each of flour, white wine vinegar, mustard and butter // 2 l (2 quarts) red wine // 0.5 l (2 cups) of chicken stock // 5 g (3 dr) of peppercorns // 5 juniper berries // 1 head of garlic

Cut the venison into small pieces and colour them in a little oil in a cast iron saucepan. Add the finely diced vegetables and the venison bones and sauté for 15 minutes. Sprinkle with the flour, then deglaze with red wine and flambé. Add the chicken stock, the peppercorns, garlic and juniper berries. Simmer for 4 hours, while skimming any scum that rises to the surface. Pour through a fine conical sieve. The following day, skim off any fat and reduce the stock. Add a little vinegar and mustard to taste, and whisk in a small amount of butter to finish.

Parmesan croquette
150 ml water (5 fl oz) // 80 g (¹/₃ cup) butter // 120 g (1 cup) flour // 3 eggs // 130 g (1 ½ cup) grated Parmesan cheese

Put the water and butter in a Thermomix and heat up to 90 °C (195 °F). Add the flour and mix rapidly, then add the eggs one by one and finish with the Parmesan cheese. Season with salt and pepper. Form quenelles with two spoons and put them in the fryer at 180 °C (360 °F) for 5 to 6 minutes.

Quince puree
Drizzle of water // 1 kg (2.2 lbs) quinces // 50 g (1.8 oz) sugar // juice of 1 lemon // 1 vanilla pod

Clean the quinces and cut into pieces, add a drizzle of water, lemon juice, sugar and the vanilla pod. Cover and cook gently. Blend and push through a conical sieve. Pour the puree into a burette and make small dots on the plate with it.

Assembly
Mushrooms and chanterelles // 1 celeriac // 1 tablespoon coarse sea salt // some Brussels sprouts

Rub the celeriac with coarse salt and bake in the oven at 220 °C (430 °F) for 1 hour. Allow to cool before cutting into cubes.

Remove the leaves from a Brussels sprout and blanch for 1 minute in boiling salted water. Drain and briefly cook them in a little butter.

Cook some Brussels sprouts in boiling salted water until al dente, cut in half and grill.

Fry the mushrooms and chanterelles in some butter and oil. Season to taste.

The intense aromas of this dish demand a beer of similar intensity. A strong quadruple will do just that, especially the dark brown Rochefort 10, the most powerful of Belgium's Trappist beers. Caramel, dried fruits, plums, raisins and yeast are the main aromas. They match perfectly with the specific taste of the deer preparation and the quince puree. www.trappistes-rochefort.com

7 TOP CHEFS CREATE A MENU FOR 21 EMBASSIES OF BELGIUM

Rome

Serves 12

The strawberries of Wépion meet Thailand ...

Strawberry and coconut medley, pistachios and yellow curry masala

// Bangkok

Given the complexity of this recipe, you should make some extra that you can save for another time.

Strawberry – vanilla sphere
Strawberry confit centre
200 g (7 oz) puree of strawberries, preferably from the Belgian village of Wépion // 30 g (1.1 oz) caster sugar // 3 g (1.7 dr) pectin NH // 8 ml (2.2 fl dr) lemon juice
Heat the puree and lemon juice together to 45 °C (113 °F). Add the sugar and pectin mixture and boil for 2 minutes. Set aside and cover completely. Cool the strawberry confit rapidly to 4 °C (39 °F) and beat with the hand mixer.

200 g (7 oz) strawberry confit // 200 g (7 oz) strawberries, diced into 5 mm (0.5 inch) cubes // 2 g (1.1 dr) lime zest // 20 ml (5.4 fl dr) lime juice
Combine the strawberries with the other ingredients, pour into spherical silicone moulds (25 mm (1 inch) diameter) and put in the freezer.

Mascarpone – vanilla coating
100 g (3.5 oz) mascarpone // 100 g (3.5 oz) whipping cream (35%) // 20 g (0.7 oz) caster sugar // ¼ vanilla pod
Make a mascarpone mousse by mixing all the ingredients together. Immediately pour this mousse into spherical silicone moulds (35 mm (1.4 inch) diameter), inserting the frozen strawberry ball into its centre. Put in the freezer. Use a colour food spray before serving to obtain a red ball.

Coconut disc
225 ml (1 cup) water // 50 g (1.8 oz) caster sugar // 25 ml (0.8 fl oz) lime juice // 10 ml (0.3 fl oz) Batida de Coco // 25 g (0.9 oz) gelatine mass
Heat the water, sugar, juice and liquor together and bring to the boil. Add the gelatine and pour onto a stainless steel tray (14 × 24 cm (5.5 × 9.4 inch)) and leave to set somewhere cool. Cut out 5 cm (2 inch) circles.

Pistachio disc
225 ml (1 cup) whipping cream (35%) // 17 g (0.6 oz) glucose // 65 g (2.3 oz) egg yolks // 50 g (1.8 oz) caster sugar // 3 g (1.7 dr) gelatine leaves // 20 g (0.7 oz) pistachio paste
Combine the cream and the glucose and bring to the boil. Whisk together the egg yolks and sugar, and add to the mixture. Cook at 83 °C (180 °F) until it coats the spoon. Remove from the heat and pass through a fine sieve. Mix in the gelatine, which has been soaked in cold water, and the pistachio paste. Beat with a hand mixer until completely smooth. Pour into 11 cm (4.3 inch) silicone disc moulds. Immediately put into the freezer. Unmould when frozen and store in a cool place.

Strawberry disc
330 g (11.6 oz) strawberry puree // 50 g (1.8 oz) caster sugar // 5 g (2.8 dr) pectin NH // 1 sheet of gelatine
Mix the sugar and pectin. Soak the gelatine in cold water. Heat the puree to 45 °C (113 °F), then add the pectin-sugar mixture. Bring to the boil while whisking and allow to boil for 2 minutes. Remove from the heat and mix in the gelatine. Immediately pour the hot jelly onto a metal sheet about 20 cm by 26 cm (8 inch × 10 inch). Allow to harden in the refrigerator and then cut out 35 and 25 mm (1.4 and 1 inch) circles.

Cushion of coconut mousse
90 g (3.2 oz) coconut puree // 16 ml (½ fl oz) Batida de Coco // 9 g (5 dr) gelatine mass // 20 g (0.7 oz) stiffly beaten egg whites // 60 g (2.1 oz) whipping cream (35%) // 100 g (3.5 oz) grated coconut
Dissolve the gelatine mass in the coconut puree. Then add the egg whites, the cream and the Batida de Coco until you get a smooth fully-combined mixture. Immediately pour the mixture to ¾ fill silicone 'stone' moulds (4 g (2.2 dr) and 8 g (4.4 dr) sizes). When set, unmould and make small cushions by laying one stone on top of another with the flat surfaces joined.

Coconut sorbet
400 g (0.9 lbs) coconut puree // 250 ml (1 cup) water // 75 g (2.6 oz) caster sugar // 40 g (1.4 oz) inverted sugar // 12 g (0.4 oz) glucose powder // 1,5 g (0.8 dr) super-neutrophil stabilizer // 1,5 g (0.8 dr) «Stab 2000» ice cream stabilizer // 10 ml (0.3 fl oz) lime juice
Bring the water and sugar to the boil and let it simmer for 1 minute. When the syrup is cold, add the stabilizers. Mix the coconut puree with the lime juice and add the syrup. Freeze in an ice cream maker for 45-60 minutes.

Coconut biscuits
100 g (3.5 oz) soft butter // 100 g (3.5 oz) caster sugar // 100 g

For this trip to Thailand, the soft, delicate aromas of strawberry and coconut can be paired with a ginger beer. Spiced beers are quite common in Belgium. They allow a great variety in aromas and subtle fragrances. **De Graal Gemberbier** will add to the Thai feel of this dish with a pronounced though not dominating ginger touch.
www.degraal.be

(3.5 oz) flour // 75 g (2.6 oz) grated coconut // 25 g (0.9 oz) almond powder // 2 g (30 gr) fleur de sel

Mix everything together and spread the mixture between 2 sheets of greaseproof paper, and roll to a thickness of 2 mm. Cut out 1 cm × 8 cm (0.4 inch × 3.1 inch) 'fingers' and freeze. Bake at 170 °C (338 °F) leaving the oven door slightly ajar to allow moisture to escape.

Yellow curry gel

100 ml (3.4 fl oz) lime juice // 100 ml (3.4 fl oz) water // 50 g (¼ cup) sugar // 5 g (2.8 dr) agar-agar // 2.5 g (1.4 dr) yellow curry masala

Heat all the ingredients at 60 °C (140 °F). Cover and set aside to infuse for 60 minutes.

Assembly

Start by putting a pistachio disc on the plate, and on top of that the strawberry vanilla sphere topped with a coconut disc. Beside this add a large and a small strawberry disc and top with a large and a small cushion of coconut mousse. Garnish the pistachio disc with small dots of yellow curry gel and coconut biscuits. Serve with a quenelle of sorbet and a line of finely diced fresh strawberries mixed with a little lime juice, caramelized pistachios and coconut chips.

Bangkok

Comme Chez Soi, housed in a superb Art Nouveau building in the centre of Brussels, is a safe bet. In 1979, it was the first restaurant outside of France to be awarded three Michelin stars. Chef Lionel Rigolet is the fourth generation of chef to make this restaurant stand out. His strong contemporary cooking is respectful of the prestigious culinary heritage handed down by his illustrious predecessor, his father-in-law, Pierre Wijnants. He is a brilliant chef who manages to remain humble in spite of a world famous clientele which includes the Belgian royal family and many famous sports stars. – **www.commechezsoi.be**

First class with a great respect for heritage

Chef Rigolet dedicates some of his classics to the **Embassies of Belgium in Washington** (USA), **Moscow** (Russia) and **The Hague** (Netherlands).

Lionel and Laurence Rigolet

Washington (USA)

Starter: Filet Américain 'Comme chez nous'

The 'filet americain préparé', or 'americain', is a classic of Belgian cuisine. This version of steak tartare, served either on bread or with a hearty portion of fries, was created by the Brussels chef, Albert Niels, at the beginning of the 19th century. It gained wider appeal at the 1935 World Expo in Brussels. Why Mr. Niels specifically chose this name is a well-kept secret. Besides, the dish is rather unusual in the United States. It is our hope that Chef Rigolet's more refined and luxurious version might be the one to tempt the American palate.

Moscow (RUSSIA)

Main dish: Veal shanks 'Art Nouveau'

Russian cuisine is always keen for a good piece of meat. Just think of beef Stroganoff or even bortsch, where a tasty veal shank can make all the difference. Chef Rigolet showcases this less well-known ingredient and allows it to take the limelight in a perfect alliance with braised Belgian endives.

The Hague (NETHERLANDS)

Dessert: Pancakes for 'Orange-Nassau'

Pancakes – a treat for the Belgians as well as the Dutch! Sweet with sugar, syrup or chocolate, or savoury like the bacon pancakes so popular in the Netherlands. Chef Rigolet dedicates his 'crêpe à l'orange' to the Dutch royal family and the House of Orange-Nassau.

Serves 4

Filet Américain 'Comme chez nous'

Steak tartare with basil and garlic

// Washington

400 g (14 oz) beef shank or shoulder // 30 g (1.1 oz) large white onion // 12 g (0.4 oz) parsley without stalks// 15 g (0.5 oz) basil leaves // 2 egg yolks // 32 g (1.1 oz) medium strong mustard // 6 g (3.3 dr) alcohol vinegar // 45 g (1.6 oz) corn oil // 0.7 g (11 gr) Worcestershire sauce // 8 g (4.5 dr) vinegar capers // 4 g (2 dr) garlic clove // 30 g (1.1 oz) small cubes of young parmesan // salt and pepper

Chop the onion and parsley and cut the basil leaves into small 7 mm (0.3 inch) squares.

In a bowl, mix the egg yolks and mustard, add a little vinegar and season. Whisk well and gradually add the corn oil, then the rest of the vinegar and finally the Worcestershire sauce. Mix everything well.

Cut and chop the meat with a knife to obtain small dice. Use a fork to add the chopped onion and parsley, capers, garlic, basil, parmesan and meat to the sauce, until you obtain a homogeneous mixture. Season and keep in the fridge.

Assembly

90 g (3.2 oz) Royal Belgian Caviar // 4 cherry tomatoes with stalk, poached and slightly pickled // 4 parmesan shavings // small basil leaves // fleur de sel // some basil oil

Place a round cutter in the centre of each plate. Divide the tartare between the different rounds, press down and smooth the surface. Put the caviar on top and gently press into place. Remove the cutters and garnish with cherry tomatoes, parmesan shavings, basil ...

This truly Belgian dish is entitled to a classic amongst the Belgian beers: **Duvel**. This world famous beer is seen as the reference among strong golden ales. It tickles the nose with peppery aromas of European hops and a beautiful yeast flavour. Duvel is known for its high carbonation and its clean and crisp mouthfeel that cuts right through the more oily components of a dish.
www.duvel.com

Washington

Serves 4

Veal shanks 'Art Nouveau'

// Moscow

Veal shanks with braised Belgian endives,
melba toast with bone marrow, potato cylinders

1 kg (2 lbs 3 oz) Belgian endives // 120 g (4.2 oz) large peeled white onions // 8 slices of veal shank (about 1,6 kg (3 ½ lbs)) // 130 g (4.6 oz) butter // 1.8 l (60 f. oz) of chicken stock // 1 sprig of fresh thyme // 1 small bay leaf // 3 cloves of garlic

Clean and wash the endives and allow to drain well. Cut into big wedges. Season the veal shanks with salt and pepper. Melt 60 g (2.1 oz) butter in a large pan. When golden brown, add the veal slices and colour them on both sides. Meanwhile, sweat the finely chopped onions in 40 g (1.4 oz) butter in a large saucepan until translucent. Add 1.5 l (50 fl oz) of the chicken stock to the pan containing the veal, and deglaze. Then add the veal and the stock to the onions. Add the thyme, bay leaf and crushed garlic. Cover and cook on low heat for about 45 minutes.

In another saucepan, melt the remaining butter. When it's foaming add the endives and cook until slightly coloured. Then add the remaining chicken stock, season and allow to simmer until just tender. The endives should retain their bite.

When the veal is almost cooked, add it to the endives. Cook the juices from the veal separately until they are reduced by half, then pour through a sieve. Add this sauce to the veal shanks and endives. Check the seasoning and stir well without breaking the veal slices.

Melba toast with bone marrow and endive

4 slices of bread // 4 marrow bones // 1 l (35 fl oz) chicken stock // 1 red endive // 1 lemon // olive oil // fleur de sel

Boil the marrow bones in a well seasoned and flavoured chicken stock. Toast the slices of bread under the grill or in the toaster and cut them into the desired size and shape. Cut 4 thick slices of bone marrow and allow to drain. Season with fleur de sel and freshly-milled pepper. Put the bone marrow on the melba toast, garnish with a julienne of red chicory seasoned with salt, pepper, lemon juice and olive oil.

Assembly

Pour some sauce into a deep plate, then add the veal shanks and finally a couple of endive wedges. Garnish with the melba toast dressed with bone marrow and endive. Serve with potato cylinders (*pomme bouchon*), garnished with some small parsley leaves and red red endive tips. Sprinkle some minced parsley and a pink peppercorn on top.

A bold Belgian 'dubbel' (the cereals used being doubled) is the perfect match for the round and buttery aromas of a rich meat dish. **Vicaris Generaal** meets all the criteria: the caramel flavours of this dark specialty beer nicely envelop the veal while its roasty malt flavours echo the mild bitterness of the Belgian endives. – www.vicaris.be

7 TOP CHEFS CREATE A MENU FOR 21 EMBASSIES OF BELGIUM

Moscow

Serves 4

Pancakes for 'Orange-Nassau' // The Hague
Caramelized orange pancakes with Liège syrup

Orange sauce
2 oranges // 50 g (1.8 oz) caster sugar // 30 g (1.1 oz) butter
Remove the zest from the oranges with a peeler, leaving behind all of the bitter white layer. Cut the zest into 30 g (1.1 oz) thin julienne. Squeeze the two oranges and reserve 200 ml (6.8 oz) of juice. Bring the juice, zest, sugar and butter to the boil in a saucepan and cook for about 10 minutes. Keep warm, lightly thickening with cornflour if necessary.

Balsamic syrup
15 g (½ oz) Liège syrup (made of apples and pears) // 4 g (2.3 dr) aged balsamic vinegar
Whisk the syrup with the balsamic vinegar and pour into a paper piping bag.

Orange tuile
75 g (2.6 oz) fresh orange juice // 265 g (9.3 oz) caster sugar // 100 g (3.5 oz) flour // 100 g (3.5 oz) melted butter // 10 g (0.35 oz) finely grated orange zest
Combine the flour and sugar in a bowl. Little by little whisk in the orange juice and zest, before adding the melted butter. Whisk to a smooth batter. Pour onto a baking sheet lined with a silicone mat and bake at 165 °C (329 °F) for 8-9 minutes. Remove from the oven, allow to cool and break in large pieces.

Pancakes
2 large eggs // 250 ml (1 cup) whole milk // 75 g (2.6 oz) flour, sifted // 100 g (3.5 oz) butter // 80 g (2.8 oz) caster sugar // a pinch of salt // 2 g (30 gr) baker's yeast // 50 ml (1.7 fl oz) Mandarine Napoleon liqueur // 24 orange segments, pith and membrane removed
Heat the milk in a saucepan until it's lukewarm. Combine a little lukewarm milk with the yeast and stir until completely dissolved. Keep the mixture warm.

Break the eggs into a bowl, whisk, add a pinch of salt, a teaspoon of sugar and the flour. Mix well and then add the warm milk and the milk-yeast mixture. Stir again. Cover the bowl with a cloth and set aside in a warm place for an hour When the batter has risen, gently stir it with a ladle taking care that it doesn't collapse too much. Heat 2 frying pans of medium size and and melt a knob of butter in each of them, taking care to spread the butter evenly. Pour a small amount of the batter into the pan, and cook over a medium heat only allowing it to colour slightly. Flip the pancakes and cook the other side in the same way. Turn the pancakes out on a rack. Take the 8 best pancakes and fold them in half.
To caramelize the pancakes, take 2 large pans, divide the remaining butter between them and melt on medium heat. Place the pancakes in the frying pans and sprinkle with half of the remaining sugar. Allow to caramelize. Flip the pancakes, sprinkle with the remaining sugar and caramelize the other side. Flip them over, flambé with the Mandarine Napoléon and remove from the heat.

Assembly
Place 2 pancakes side by side on each warmed plate. Pour the caramel remaining in the frying pans over the pancakes, dividing it equally between them. Then drizzle with 2 tablespoons of the orange sauce. Arrange the lukewarm orange wedges and zest on top, and decorate the edge of the plate with alternating dots of balsamic syrup and orange sauce. Finally add the orange tuiles.

Although this dessert goes with every season, we suggest a sturdy winter beer: **Tsjeeses**. The malted and bittersweet backbone nicely supports the sweet orange flavour. The harmony is even further enhanced by the beautiful orange glow of this beer. – **www.struise.com**

7 TOP CHEFS CREATE A MENU FOR 21 EMBASSIES OF BELGIUM

LIONEL AND LAURENCE RIGOLET

The Hague

Beer, the ambassador of Belgian diversity

.be our guest

BEER, THE AMBASSADOR OF BELGIAN DIVERSITY

Many beer enthusiasts regard Belgium as the home of beer. Being an intrinsic part of Belgian DNA, it is also recognised by UNESCO, which has put Belgian beer culture on its Intangible Cultural Heritage list.

Beer is as old as civilization itself. It was the common drink in Western Europe, until the Romans gradually progressed to wine. They associated beer with 'barbarians', such as the *Belgae* … And this idea that drinking wine is more civilised than drinking beer would persist for many centuries to come … But today that statement no longer applies, in fact the opposite is true.

In this region the rise of this amber-coloured elixir goes back to the monks and nuns of the Middle Ages. They brewed table beer (a light version for the nuns and the ordinary people, and a stronger version for the monks themselves) because the drinking water was often contaminated and made people sick. They added herbs to vary the taste and hops to allow it to be stored for longer.

The various traditional production methods have been carefully passed down from generation to generation, each further enhancing and refining the beer. *Rochefort, Rodenbach, Achel, Chimay, Duvel, Gulden Draak, Hoegaarden, Leffe, Maredsous, Orval, Westmalle, Corsendonk, De Koninck* … these are just a few of the traditional beers that are still available today, and which have given Belgian beers such prominence worldwide. Meanwhile, in parallel, there is an increasing number of high-quality 'newcomers'. Over the past twenty years there has been a new vibrancy in the beer sector, with young, passionate brewers, trendy micro-breweries and a new generation of beer drinkers particularly fond of specialty beers. Modern techniques and fresh ingredients, combined with traditional know-how, have given rise to the next generation of outstanding brewers. The University of Leuven, the city where the world's biggest brewery AB Inbev has its registered seat, even offers an academic course on the 'technology of beer brewing'!

But what is it that actually makes Belgian beer culture so unique? It can be summarised in one word: diversity! No country in the world offers so many different styles of beer. And, on top of that, within each beer style there are countless beers, over 1500 Belgian beers in total, with about 700 different taste profiles and varying alcohol percentages. From high fermentation to low, and from spontaneous to mixed, from light to dark and from sweet to sour. From ordinary Pils to Trappist beers, from dark beers through red and golden to white beers, from the cloudy and slightly sour Gueuze-Lambic to the more alcoholic Tripel and Quadrupel … There is something for everyone.

Because the range of Belgian beers perfectly reflects the diversity of the country, with its different languages and cultures, Belgian beer is the perfect ambassador of Belgian diversity to bring to your dining table. Cheers!

BELGIAN BEER FOR DUMMIES

Which types of beer should you be able to recognise?

Pils / Lager: This is the most popular beer type and includes *Stella Artois, Jupiler, Maes, Primus, Cristal, Vedett* … They all have a light golden colour with a distinctive taste of hops.

Trappist: Different styles of beer brewed by Cistercian monks in six abbeys in Belgium: *Achel, Chimay, Orval, Rochefort, Westmalle,* and *Westvleteren*. Notably, the Westvleteren 12 was voted the best beer in the world by RateBeer for several years in a row. In total, there are currently only 11 Trappist beers in the world.

Abbey beer or monastery beer: Collective name for beers with a monastic origin but brewed outside the monastery walls: for example *Sint-Bernardus, Ename, Grimbergen, Tongerlo, Straffe Hendrik, Maredsous, Leffe, Floreffe, Aulne, Villers, Corsendonk* … The most famous versions are either the relatively dark brown and sweet 'dubbel', or the sharper, and usually heavier blonde 'tripel'.

White beer: White beer is an unfiltered cloudy wheat beer with hints of coriander and orange zest. Its ancestors are the beers from the medieval duchy of Brabant. Examples include *Hoegaarden, Brugs* or *St. Bernardus white beer, Blanche de Namur* …

Lambic & Gueuze: Lambic is a deep gold to amber-coloured flat beer derived from spontaneous fermentation, which gives the beer its special, sharper and more sour taste. Lambic is one of the oldest Belgian beer styles and originates from the Brussels region. Gueuze is produced by mixing young and old lambic together. In this category you will find *Mort Subite, Belle-Vue, Boon, Cantillon, Lindemans, Tilquin, 3 Fonteinen* … Also the sweet fruity Kriek Lambic is very popular. Cherries (kriek) are added to lambic before it is completely fermented, giving an extra boost to the process while the cherry kernels add woody notes (*Oude Kriek 3 Fonteinen*). Other types of fruit are also used to make variations on this beer type.

Specialty beer: All other unclassified beers are commonly called specialty beers. Their taste varies greatly, ranging from sweet to bitter, spicy to fruity, light to strong. Think of *Bourgogne des Flandres, Brugse Zot, Delirium Tremens, Duchesse de Bourgogne, Kasteelbier, La Chouffe, Liefmans Goudenband, Lucifer, Omer, Reserve Royale* …

Which beer in which season?

Heavy, dark beers are considered to be winter beers. Summer beers should be fresh and more accessible. The most refreshing summer beer type is white beer, but the classic lagers also do very well. In addition, more and more light specialty beers – even non-alcoholic ones – are appearing on the market and are perfect for hot summer days.

Food pairing

Beer and food pairings are increasingly popular. Beer has a lot more flavour components and varieties than wine, which makes beer more interesting for a refined pairing. This is particularly true in combinations with cheese, where beer definitely takes the lead. In other areas, white beer works very well with mussels, while dark beers are better suited to meat dishes and fruit beers are ideal for desserts. Top chefs are increasingly inclined to put specialty beers on the menu while bartenders use all kinds of beers when creating cocktails. Meanwhile, courses for beer brewing and for beer sommeliers are extremely popular. Beer is really in vogue!

In Chapter III where 7 top chefs cook for 21 Embassies of Belgium, Daniella Provost suggests pairings with a selection of beers including *Saison Dupont, Vicaris Generaal, Cuvée des Trolls, L'Arogante, Malheur Brut, Duvel, De Graal Gember, Ardenne Stout, Caulier 28 Saison, Bertinchamps Tripel, Gouden Carolus Tripel, Tsjeeses, Corsendonk Agnus, St. Bernardus Abt 12, Blanche de Namur, Réserve Royale, Orval, Delirium Tremens, Rochefort 10, Oude kriek 3 Fonteinen, Westmalle Dubbel* and *Mariage Parfait*.

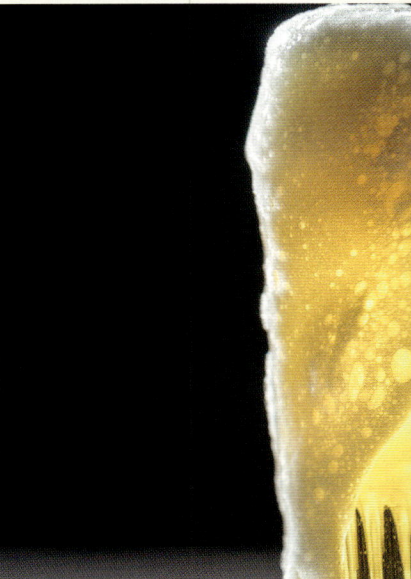

Some beer sayings:

'Beer after wine and you'll feel fine; wine after beer and you'll feel queer' or is it the opposite?
'Beer on wine not so fine; wine on beer, never fear': Who knows the answer?

It's small beer: It's not important

Life is not all beer and skittles: Not everything in life can be fun.

To cry in one's beer: To feel sorry for oneself.

I've seen better heads on nickel beers: To suggest that someone is not very clever.

Champagne tastes on a beer budget: A person with expensive tastes but a low salary.

Adam's ale is an old-fashioned term for plain water.

Beer money is money that's left over after the essentials are paid for and can be used for treats or luxuries, such as beer.

And to conclude, according to William Shakespeare in A Winter's Tale, *'a quart of ale is a dish for a king'*.

Daniella Provost

The psychology of Belgian beer

Daniella Provost is a psychologist with a passion for beer. As an occasional guide in a Belgian brewery, the brewing process no longer holds any secrets for her. Daniella conducts beer tasting and food pairing events and loves to interact with other beer lovers and brewers to learn more about the history and culture of their beers. In her capacity as a certified 'beer connoisseur' and Cicerone, or beer sommelier, she is sometimes asked to join official trade missions abroad. Beer is a passion that transcends borders and brings people from all cultures and backgrounds closer together.
www.belgianzythologist.be

In Chapter III, Daniella pairs the 21 dishes of our 7 top chefs to Belgian specialty beers.

BEER ON YOUR BUFFET TABLE

Your buffet table will inspire even more hospitality when you have Belgian beers to offer. You can of course consider classics such as Stella, Cristal, Jupiler, Kriek beer, Duvel, Leffe, Hoegaarden, Chimay, Corsendonk … but definitely some of the less well known specialty beers as well. We suggest the following beers, which have been declared in recent years to be 'the best beer in the world' in their category. They include even gluten-free and veggie varieties!

In the category 'World's Best Dark Beer'
Best Old Brown:
- Liefmans Goudenband, www.liefmans.be
- Rodenbach Grand Cru en Rodenbach Vintage, www.rodenbach.be
- Vander Ghinste Oud Bruin, www.omervanderghinste.be
- Queue de Charrue Oud Bruin, www.vanuxeem.com

Belgian Style Strong:
- Cuvée Clarisse, www.brouwerijwilderen.be
- Leffe Radieuse, www.leffe.com

In the category 'World's Best Flavoured Beer'
Spirit Flavoured Beer:
- Gouden Carolus, Cuvée van de Keizer Whisky infused, www.hetanker.be

Fruit Flavoured Beer:
- Rodenbach Rosso, www.palm.be

Fruit & Vegetable Flavoured Beer:
- Rodenbach Caractere Rouge, www.palm.be

Gose / Other Sour Beer:
- Petrus Aged Pale, www.brouwerijdebrabandere.be

In the category 'World's Best Pale Beer'
Belgian Style Pale Ale:
- Seef's Bootje's Bier and Seefbier, www.seef.be

Belgian Style Tripel:
- Affligem Tripel, www.affligembeer.com
- Bersalis Tripel, www.oudbeersel.com
- Gouden Carolus Tripel, www.hetanker.be
- Tripel Kanunnik, www.brouwerijwilderen.be

Belgian Style Blonde:
- Affligem Blond and Affligem Hop Selection, www.affligembeer.com
- Fagnes Blond, www.brasseriedesfagnes.com
- Leffe Blonde, www.leffe.com
- Moat, www.moat.be
- Omer Traditional Blond, www.bockor.be
- Paljas, www.paljas-beer.com
- Palm Royale, www.palm.be
- Queue de Charrue Blond, www.vanuxeem.com
- Réserve Royale, www.reserveroyale.com
- Tongerlo Blond, www.haacht.com
- Wilderen Goud, www.brouwerijwilderen.be

Belgian Style Strong:
- Gouden Carolus Cuvée Van De Keizer Rood, www.hetanker.be
- Leffe Rituel and Leffe Royale, www.leffe.com

Amber:
- Queue de Charrue Ambrée, www.vanuxeem.com

Bière De Garde / Saison:
- Paljas Saison, www.paljas-beer.com

In the category 'World's Best Sour Beer'
Lambic:
- Mort Subite Oude Gueuze Lambic, www.mort-subite.be

Flavoured Lambic:
- Lindemans Blossom Gueuze, www.lindemans.be
- Quetsche Tilquin à l'ancienne, www.gueuzerietilquin.be

Gueuze:
- Mort Subite Oude Gueuze, www.mort-subite.be
- Oud Beersel Oude Gueuze, www.oudbeersel.com
- Timmermans Tradition Oude Gueuze, anthonymartin.be

Kriek:
- Mort Subite Kriek Lambic Tradition, www.mort-subite.be

In the category 'World's Best Specialty Beer'
Brut / Champagne Beer:
- Oud Beersel Bzart Lambiek, www.oudbeersel.com

Gluten-free Beer:
- Brunehaut Triple and Brunehaut Blonde, www.brunehaut.com
- St-Feuillien Grisette Blonde Sans Gluten Bio, www.st-feuillien.com

Rice Beer:
- Betty B., www.bossuwebrewing.com

.be our guest

7 simple dishes for a walking dinner

'Brusseleir' – born and raised in Brussels – Albert Verdeyen is above all a true Belgian: perfectly bilingual, loved as much in the north as in the south of the country, charming, entrepreneurial and full of humour. Albert knows how to hit the right chord with many people, not only because of his warm personality, but especially because of his simple yet very tasty cuisine. He has a preference for authentic and popular dishes, with a special focus on the 'stoemp' – mashed potato with which you can combine almost anything. He stands for a kitchen that evokes family security, a coming-home-feeling and youth nostalgia. But Albert's no-nonsense approach makes it at the same time completely in line with the latest food trends!
albertverdeyen@gmail.com – www.vanzovi.be

Master chef of authentic popular cuisine and stoemp

With much love and expertise, Chef Albert has prepared 7 simple dishes referring to Belgian specialties. Ideal when you expect a lot of people or prefer a more informal buffet formula. But these cool dishes are also a perfect serve at the kitchen table.

Albert Verdeyen

Cod fillet with pickles sauce
Cod is a tasty fish from the North Sea with beautiful bright white and firm meat. You can prepare it in every possible way: in the oven, grilled, baked, poached, in papillote, steamed … Try also the Belgian pickles sauce! Less sweet than its Anglo-Saxon cousin, this typical sauce not only gives fish, but also fries and meat guaranteed more character.

Asparagus puffs
White asparagus is a Belgian delicacy. There are numerous methods of preparation, including the classic recipe: 'Asparagus Flemish style', with butter sauce, parsley, nutmeg and crushed boiled eggs. If you would like to serve it as finger food or on a buffet, a puff pastry comes in handy. Or how 'tasty' can be so very simple …

Coucou de Malines with Ardennes ham
Chicken comes in all sizes and qualities. One of those winged creatures to be proud of is the Malines cuckoo, a juicy Belgian chicken. Chef Verdeyen prepares a roulade: the soft, sweet meat is wrapped in smoked Ardennes ham and filled with creamy fresh cheese. To lick your thumbs and fingers!

Endive croquettes
Once upon a time there was an ugly chicory root that grew into beautiful white leaves ('witloof' in Flemish) … It sounds like a fairy tale, but it is a true success story. Around 1850, the surprising effect of growing in the dark was discovered in a basement in Brussels. This beautiful vegetable was born and has since become an integral part of Belgian cuisine. Chef Verdeyen makes his favorite 'stoemp' (potato-based) croquette, a bite with no complexes to simply enjoy.

Mussels croquettes
Mussels with fries can be considered to be the national dish of Belgium. And one of the most popular hot starters is definitely the shrimp croquette prepared with the refined North Sea shrimps. Chef Verdeyen has difficulty choosing between both toppers, so he combines the best of both worlds and proposes a tasty mussel croquette. Pure or with a mussel sauce, it's up to you.

Royal stoemp with lobster
A lobster from time to time is the ideal ingredient for a luxurious gourmet meal. For a most memorable stoemp, all you need is some fresh herbs and a piece of deliciously prepared lobster. On a walking dinner it is a bite with royal grandeur.

Flemish beef stew
No, we have not forgotten the Flemish beef stew, which together with fries is an intrinsic part of Belgian culinary heritage. The combination of beer and beef gives a special flavor to this iconic dish. This is a must for beer lovers! And certainly also for real fries lovers!

Basic preparation for all kinds of 'stoemp'

1 kg (2 lbs 3 oz) potatoes serves 4 to 6

Peel and wash the potatoes. Chef Verdeyen uses mainly 'bintjes', which are perfectly suited to make stoemp. Cook the potatoes in a large pot of salted water. Prick the potatoes with a sharp little knife and if there is no resistance, they are cooked. Drain and pass through a food mill or crush with a potato masher without adding fat (neither milk, butter, eggs, nor cream).
Keep in the fridge. It will be useful when you have little time to cook.

Serves about 10

Cod fillet with pickles sauce

on a bed of mashed potatoes with white chocolate

300 g (10.6 oz) cod fillet or other firm white fish // 1 tablespoon butter // 150 ml (5 fl oz) water // 3 tablespoons pickles sauce with chunks (also called Blackwell sauce) // 250 ml (8.5 fl oz) cream // finely chopped parsley // 200 g (7 oz) mashed potatoes // 20 g (0.7 oz) white chocolate

Melt the butter over a medium heat until hazelnut brown and foamy. Season the fish, put it in the pan and cook for 2 to 3 minutes, depending on its thickness. Turn the fish over and cook the other side for another 3 minutes. Remove the fish from the pan and allow to rest under aluminum foil.
Deglaze the pan with 150 ml (5 fl oz) of water. Whisk to release what's sticking on the bottom of the pan. Then add 3 tablespoons of pickles sauce and the cream. Cook and reduce until the sauce is thickened. Serve the sauce together with the fish and garnish with some chopped parsley.
Meanwhile, heat the mashed potatoes and add the chocolate. Mix until smooth and serve together with the fish.

Serves about 10

Asparagus puffs

1 puff pastry sheet // 100 g (3.5 oz) grated cheese // curry powder, salt, pepper // 1 egg // butter // ½ bunch of white asparagus (from Mechelen)

Preheat the oven to 180 °C (356 °F). Cut the pastry into neat squares of 5 cm by 5 cm (2 inch × 2 inch). Brush with a little beaten egg and bake for 15 to 20 minutes in the oven until golden brown.

Meanwhile, peel the asparagus and cut into small pieces. Fry in a pan with butter until they are *al dente*. Season with salt and pepper and a pinch of curry powder.
Remove the pastry from the oven and open the squares as pictured. Put a few pieces of warm asparagus in each square and sprinkle with grated cheese and the curry jus of the asparagus.

Serves 10

Coucou de Malines with Ardennes ham

2 chicken fillets (preferably Coucou de Malines) // 150 g (5 oz) spinach, cut in slices // 90 g (3.2 oz) fresh cottage cheese // 4 slices of smoked ham (preferably Ardennes ham // ½ zucchini // 100 ml (3.4 fl oz) water

Open the fillets by making a deep horizontal cut in each fillet (don't slice completely).
Put 80 g (2.8 oz) of cottage cheese and spinach in a bowl and mix. Season with pepper and salt.
Spread the spinach-cheese mixture over the four chicken fillets and roll tightly. You can also use herb cheese for the filling.
Carefully wrap each chicken breast with two slices of ham so that they are completely packed. If necessary, stick in a toothpick to keep everything together.
Melt some butter in a frying pan, and cook the chicken breasts on both sides until golden brown.
Deglaze with water and put a lid on the pan. Allow to simmer for 10 minutes on a low heat.
In the meantime, slice the zucchini and grill in the oven.
For the sauce: Remove the chicken fillets from the pan and add the rest of the cottage cheese to the gravy. Allow to simmer for 2 minutes. Season with salt and pepper.
Assembly: Cut the filet into slices and put them on a slice of grilled zucchini. Drizzle some sauce on top.

TIP: As a Main dish, you can serve with fried potatoes and a bowl of fresh lettuce and tomatoes. The best fried potatoes are made with potatoes that were cooked the day before.

Serves 10

Endive croquettes

500 g (1.1 lbs) potatoes // 6 endives (chicory) // 50 g (1.8 oz) butter // nutmeg // flour // 1 egg // breadcrumbs // pepper and salt

Make a basic purée of mashed potatoes (see p. 150). Cut the endives into small pieces and fry with some butter. Allow to simmer and season. Depending on your taste, you can opt for crunchy, al dente or cooked. If you have a sweet tooth, you can also add a pinch of sugar, especially if the endive tastes bitter.

Add the cooked endive pieces to the mashed potatoes and mix well. Make balls using two tablespoons. Allow to harden in the fridge overnight.
Roll the croquettes in flour, then in egg yolk and breadcrumbs. Fry at 160 °C (320 °F) until golden brown.
This simple croquette is surprisingly tasty and lends itself perfectly as finger food during a reception, accompanied by a mustard sauce. It can also be served with a good piece of meat.

TIP: The endives can be replaced by, for example, asparagus, Brussels sprouts or other vegetables of your choice. If the vegetables are quite hard, boil them first for about 5 minutes in salted water with a spoonful of sherry vinegar. Then proceed as in this recipe. If you want to enhance the vegetable taste, boil the potatoes in the water of the vegetables.

Serves 10

Mussels croquettes

Croquettes
500 g (1.1 lbs) North Sea mussels // 150 ml (5.1 fl oz) dry white wine // 1 onion // 1 celery // 3 l (3 quarts) milk // 2 gelatine sheets // 80 g (2.8 oz) butter // olive oil // 120 g (4.2 oz) flour // 100 g (3.5 oz) grated cheese // 2 eggs // breadcrumbs // 1 lemon // parsley

Scrape and clean the mussels thoroughly with cold water. Sauté the onion and chopped celery with a little olive oil in a large deep frying pan. Add the mussels and white wine. Cook the mussels with the lid on the pan for about 5 minutes. Shake the pan from time to time so that they all reach the same temperature and open up. Take the mussels from the pan and pass the broth through a fine sieve.
Pour the milk into a saucepan and add ½ litre of the mussels broth. Allow to simmer over low heat for about 20 minutes, then add the gelatine previously soaked and drained.
Make a roux with butter and flour and add the milk little by little over low heat. Stir well and cook until the sauce has thickened. Add the chopped mussels and season. Finally, add the grated cheese and mix well until the cheese is completely dissolved.
Take a deep container lightly coated with olive oil and pour in the mixture. Put in the fridge and allow to rest overnight.
The next day, roll small croquettes with wet hands. Roll them in the flour, then in a soup plate with egg yolk and finally toss them in breadcrumbs. Fry at 180 °C (356 °F).

Sauce for the mussel croquettes
3 tablespoons mayonnaise // 3 tablespoons mustard // 2 tablespoons yogurt // tarragon vinegar // salt and pepper

Mix the mayonnaise with mustard and yogurt. Season with a dash of tarragon vinegar, a pinch of salt and some freshly ground pepper.
Serve the croquettes with sauce, a lemon wedge and fried parsley.

Serves 10

Royal stoemp with lobster and fine herbs from the garden

Stoemp with fine herbs
250 g (8.8 oz) of mashed potatoes (see p. 150) // chervil // chives // parsley // 1 to 2 tablespoons olive oil // salt and pepper

Blend the herbs and olive oil and add to the mashed potatoes according to your taste. Be careful not add too much if you still want to enjoy the taste of lobster. Also, nutmeg is not recommended in this stoemp recipe because it will be too dominant. Mix and adjust the seasoning.

Lobster
1 lobster (cut in half) // butter // 2 tablespoons of flour // 1 tablespoon harissa // cayenne pepper // 3 tablespoons olive oil // 1 shallot // 2 garlic cloves // salt and pepper // ½ bunch of parsley // 250 ml (8.5 fl oz) tomato coulis // fresh tarragon

Use the back of your knife to crack the lobster claws. Remove the lobster's intestines. Season with pepper and salt. Remove the lobster's brain and put it in a bowl. Add some butter, harissa and a pinch of cayenne pepper.
Melt butter and olive oil in a pan and cook the lobster, starting with the meat side down. Put the lid on the pan and allow to cook for a minute.
Finely slice the shallot and crush the garlic. Remove the stems from the parsley. Turn the lobster and add the chopped vegetables. Add some water and steam for one minute.
Place the lobster on an oven plate and put the brain mixture back into the lobster's head. Drizzle some olive oil over the lobster and bake in the preheated oven at 180 °C (356 °F) for 5 to 7 minutes. Add the cooked vegetables with the flour to the pan and then pour in the tomato coulis. Finely chop the tarragon and add to the coulis.
Remove the lobster from the oven, dissect and cut the flesh into thick slices.

Assembly
Heat the mashed potatoes. Put the lobster pieces in the pan with the sauce and add the brains mixture to the coulis. Put some stoemp on a plate and arrange the lobster pieces on top. Pass the coulis and leftovers through a fine sieve and serve with this sauce.

Serves 10

Flemish beef stew with fries and mayonnaise

Flemish Beef Stew
500 g (1.1 lbs) of beef (chuck or beef shank) // butter // 2 tablespoons flour // 1 bottle of fairly sweet Belgian brown beer // 200 ml (6.8 fl oz) water // 1 tablespoon beef broth // 2 onions // thyme // 3 bay leaves // 2 tablespoons brown sugar // mustard

Cut the beef into equal cubes. Heat the butter in a pan and brown the beef cubes on all sides. Season with pepper and salt. Sprinkle one tablespoon of flour over the beef. Then put the meat in a deep casserole pan and sprinkle another tablespoon of flour over it.
Peel and roughly dice the onions. Sauté the onions together with the sugar in the fat of the meat until soft and golden brown. Then add a little water, bring to the boil and scrape the brown bits from the bottom of the pan.
Add the onions to the casserole pan with the meat. Next, pour in the beer and the beef broth (not cold so as not to 'grab' the meat). Add thyme, bay leaves and mustard and bring to the boil, then reduce heat and simmer for 60 to 90 minutes. Do not put a lid on it. The cooking time depends on the quality of the meat. Stir from time to time in the pan and check whether the meat is sufficiently cooked. Put the lid on as soon as the sauce has the desired thickness.

This typical Belgian dish is preferably served with homemade chips and a large spoonful of mayonnaise.

Belgian Fries / Frites / Chips
1 kg (2.2 lbs) of floury potatoes (such as Bintje) // 4 l (7 pints) vegetable oil resistant to high temperature or beef fat // salt

Peel the potatoes, wash and cut them by hand into fries. The ideal Belgian frie is 1 cm (0.4 inch) thick and 6-7 cm (2 ½ inch) long. Do not wash the fries so that the starch is not removed. Bake the fries two times: First, at 140 °C - 160 °C (280 °F - 320 °F), where the chips begin to cook, but not brown. Let the fries cool and drain on a cooling rack or kitchen paper. Bake them a second time at 180 °C (356 °F) until crisp and golden. Drain the fries well when cooked. Then let your guests add salt and mayonnaise at will.

7 SIMPLE DISHES FOR A WALKING DINNER

Receptions

Belgian fries, an ambassador of Belgian unity

.be our guest

'Friteries' or snack kiosks selling freshly-cooked fries (chips), are very typically Belgian and therefore a sure symbol of Belgitude. With more than 5,000 friteries (also known as fritures or fritkots), Belgium is unique in the world. Almost every town, district and village has one, a place for people of all ranks, Walloon and Fleming alike, regulars as well as the casual passers-by to meet at almost any time of the day (and night) while standing in the queue for a steaming bag of fries. This is about so much more than just popular gastronomy. The appetite for fries seems to be in the genes of every Belgian. For example, in many households there is a 'fries day', a fixed – almost ritual – day in the week when the family will go to the friterie. Often after a night out – a football match, a cycling competition or a concert – going to the friterie is the logical conclusion to a beautiful evening. Together or alone, in a paper cone or out of a cardboard box, using fingers or a fork, with mayonnaise or chilli-hot samourai sauce, accompanied by some Flemish beef stew or frikandel meatballs, at 'Friture Billie and Kiki' or 'Maison Antoine', everyone has their own preferences and their favourite friterie, which has been carefully selected based on the taste and crispness of the fries, its location, service and atmosphere. Contrary to every kind of modern logic, a friterie should be low on frills and publicity, but full of personality and human warmth, as well as a touch of nostalgia. This bizarre phenomenon is the cornerstone of Belgian 'fritkot culture', a tradition that has existed for centuries, and which has been recognised in Belgium as a part of its intangible cultural heritage. It is something to cherish. Every year there is a national Belgian fries week; and in Bruges you can find the only museum in the world devoted to the Belgian fry. Belgians do not mind the 'fries humour', a genre mainly practised by the French and the Dutch to make fun of them. The only thing that might upset them, is that so many English speakers stubbornly continue to call Belgian fries, the ambassador of Belgian unity, 'French' fries …

We also have a real-life Ambassador of Belgian Fries – James Bint, who owes his name to the bintje potato, one of the best for making frites. His mission? 'A licence to fry!'
– jamesbint.be

.be our guest

7 healthy recipes for a business lunch

Arabelle Meirlaen

'I think of my cooking in the same way I think of life: beautiful, flavoursome, pithy, filled with love and emotions ...', that is what it says on the homepage of Arabelle Meirlaen's restaurant of the same name, located close to Huy. Arabelle is a rare flower in the predominantly male world of top chefs. Completely unflappable, she follows her own intuitive gastronomic path, in tune with her body and nature's seasons. In this way she is inspired to create delicate and balanced dishes which excite the taste buds, and which in all their beauty could only be the work of a woman's hand. But above all, this is healthy food. Arabelle's deep interest in the beneficial properties of plants and herbs is a common thread running through her amazing culinary repertoire. This connoisseur of the 21st century has a clear message: be what you eat, indulge yourself while respecting your own body and above all ... stay zen. – **www.arabelle.be**

Healthy and intuitive cuisine with a feminine touch

Chef Arabelle, former Female Chef of the Year, shares seven of her favourite recipes. They are very suitable for a quick and healthy business lunch. Arabelle would like to dedicate them to **Princess Astrid**, who, at the King's request, represents him on **trade missions abroad**. These missions are always co-organised by the **Embassies of Belgium** in cooperation with the three regional export agencies. Our Princess leads these missions with a warm-hearted dynamism and an enthusiasm which finds its equal in the passion of Chef Arabelle.

Healthy business menu

A pair of drinks 'Mens sana in corpore sano': It is difficult to choose between birch juice from the mythical Northern birch tree, and Kombucha, the Far Eastern 'elixir of immortality'. Both drinks are invigorating and will surely bring positive energy to any lunch, whether for business or for pleasure.

Spring rolls: In the spring, green shoots and antioxidants have a beneficial and purifying effect on our body. These fairytale vegetable rolls with their chlorophyll green sauce give a boost to every businessman or woman.

Mosaic of summer tomatoes: A simple but eye-catching little dish for every occasion. An antioxidant treatment to oil the wheels of any business conversation that might stall.

'Ayurvedic' lobster from the Belgian coast: Ayurvedic spices such as turmeric, cardamom, cumin, cinnamon and ginger are of great importance in Arabelle's healthy cooking. They leave you feeling completely 'Zen' …

Back to the roots: This wok of garden roots is a winter dish that adds warmth and depth to cold negotiations. And einkorn wheat, which completes this dish, is an ancestor of modern wheat and low in gluten.

Vegan cheese platter: Don't let lactose intolerance get in the way of your business deal.

A fragrance of 3 fruits: This multi-layered arrangement of flavours inspired by an artisan perfume from Namur, will take not only your eyes, but also your nose, on a voyage of discovery. The ideal dessert for those with a nose for business.

A pair of drinks 'Mens sana in corpore sano'

Birch sap with citrus fruits
The birch is a mysterious tree from the north which features in many myths and sagas. No other tree is as robust as the birch; it grows in even the furthest reaches of the Arctic Circle. It is sacred to the Siberians who believe that a man's strength increases tenfold when he drinks its sap. For the Germanic peoples, it is the tree of wisdom. They attribute magical and medicinal properties to its leaves, twigs and sap. The Celts dedicate the birch to Brigit, goddess of medicine. Celtic druids used its twigs during their initiation rites. In Norway, Sweden, Scotland and parts of England, houses are still decorated with birch branches during the summer solstice (21 June). Therefore it is not surprising that birch sap is known in herbal medicine for its purifying properties. Ideally, a 21-day treatment should be undertaken in the spring and autumn.

1l (1 quart) birch sap taken in spring (by attaching a can under a wedge-shaped incision in the trunk's southwesterly side – 1 incision per tree for no longer than a week – if necessary, the sap can be frozen) // 1 tablespoon honey // 10 organic kumquats or other citrus fruits
Cut the fruit into slices and mix everything. Allow to infuse for 10 days in the fridge, then strain and bottle. This drink can be stored for up to a year in the fridge.

Kombucha
Kombucha is also known as the 'immortal elixir' in China. Originating from the Far East 2000 years ago, this sparkling tea is reputed to have multiple beneficial effects on health. There are few ingredients in kombucha, mainly just tea and sugar. But in reality it's a little more complicated. In order to ferment the liquid, a symbiotic culture of bacteria and yeast (SCOBY), a kombucha mother, is needed. It must either be obtained from someone who makes his own kombucha, or can be ordered online. Arabelle's recipe is as follows:

1 l (1 quart) mineral water // 2 tablespoons each black and green tea // 100 g (3.5 oz) honey or cane sugar // Kombucha mother (SCOBY)
Heat the water with the tea, add the honey, allow to cool to room temperature and add the kombucha mushrooms.

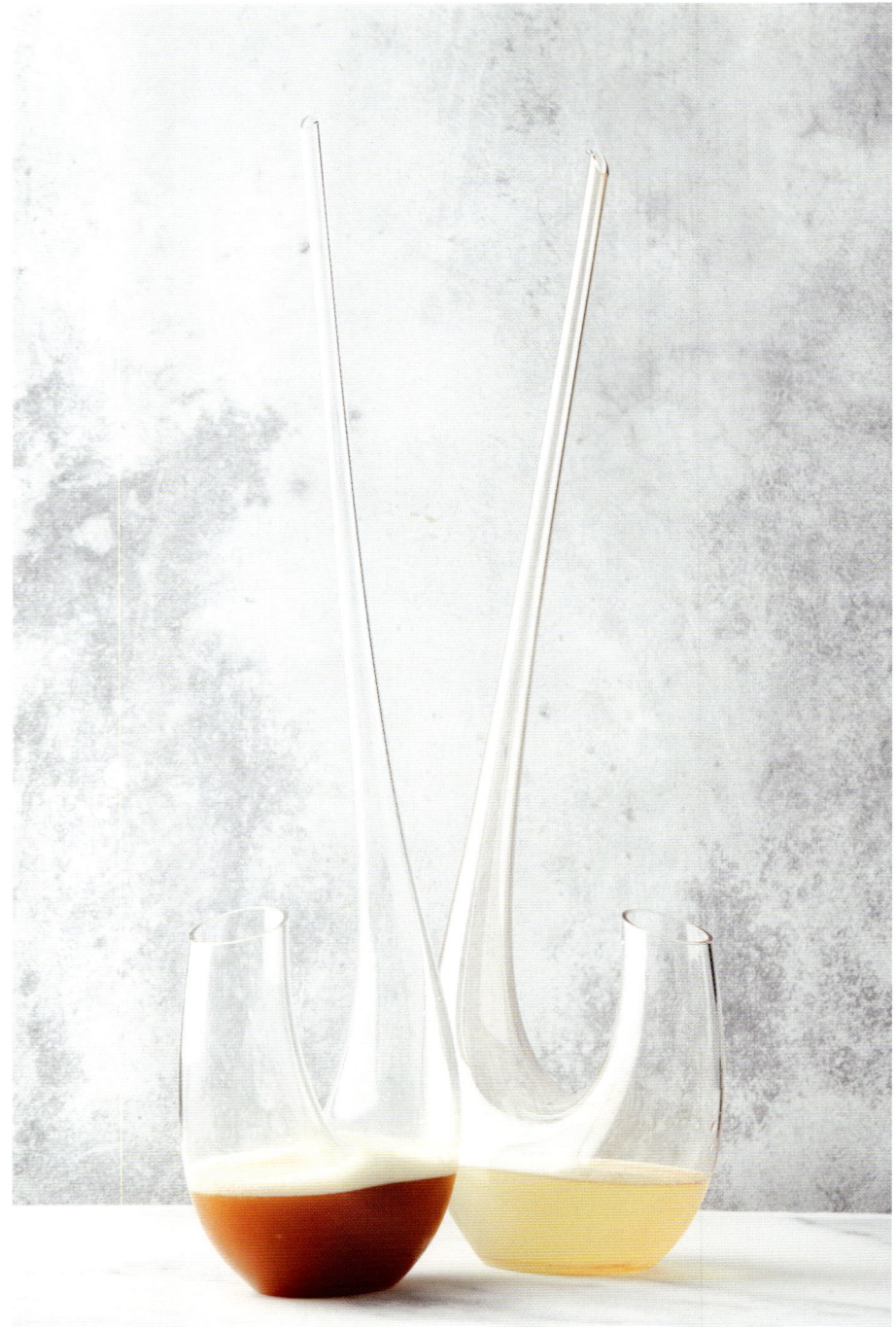

Then leave to ferment for 7 – 15 days at 20-25 °C (68-77 °F) in a jar covered with a cloth that allows for fermentation, which will result in a sparkling drink. Strain through a sieve, bottle and put in the cellar. You can mix the kombucha with fruit juices to soften its rather pronounced taste.

Serves 4

Spring rolls

Vegetable rolls with green vegetable sauce

The marinade
50 ml (1.7 oz) rice vinegar or white wine vinegar // 100 ml (3.4 fl oz) water // 40 g (1.4 oz) caster sugar // 50 g (1.8 oz) shallots // 20 g (0.7 oz) fresh ginger // 20 fresh coriander leaves // 2 cm (0.8 inch) bird's eye chilli

Finely chop the peeled ginger along with the shallots, coriander and chilli. Mix together all the ingredients in a bowl, allow to rest for 30 minutes, then strain.

Vegetable rolls
200 g (7 oz) black radish // 200 g (7 oz) yellow beetroots // 200 g (7 oz) kohlrabi or daikon // 200 g (7 oz) large orange carrots // 200 g (7 oz) chioggia or red beetroot

Scrub all the vegetables and finely slice into 1 mm (0.04 inch) lengths, using a mandoline or slicer. Marinate the vegetables for at least 30 minutes, but no more than 12 hours, then drain. Place two slices of each vegetable one on top of the other and roll tightly.

Vegetable sauce
40 g (1.4 oz) carrot tops // 2 lemon verbena leaves // 3.5 g (2 dr) fresh ginger // 3.5 g (2 dr) fresh coriander // 60 ml (2 fl oz) tangerine juice // 25 ml (3.4 fl oz) extra virgin olive oil // 1 pinch of sea salt // 15 ml (0.5 fl oz) cider vinegar // 45 ml (1.5 fl oz) water // ½ tablespoon honey or caster sugar

Wash the carrot tops and coriander and peel the ginger. Put all the ingredients in a food processor and blend to a smooth sauce. Store in the fridge in a hermetically sealed jar.

Assembly
Pour the sauce carefully onto the plate. Cut the rolls in half and place 6 rolls on each plate. Garnish according to taste, for example with coriander flowers. Or you could make spring onion curls for a nice decorative touch: roll a green spring onion stalk, then finely cut lengthwise into 1-2 mm (0.04 – 0.08 inch) wide strips. Put in iced water for a few minutes until they form curls.

Tomato mosaic

Garden tomatoes with elderberry juice

Elderberry syrup
10 clusters black elderberries // 5 tablespoons cane sugar or honey
Wash the berries, then top and tail. Put them in a saucepan with the sugar or honey and a few teaspoons of water. Stir and cook for a few minutes, then strain through a stainless steel tamis. Bottle while the syrup is still hot. Store in the cellar or fridge.

Tomato salad
Different varieties of tomato: green zebra, beef heart, sweetheart, champagne cherry, pineapple, black oxheart, pear, sungold cherry ... // extra virgin olive oil // pinch of fleur de sel // mixed peppercorns in a mill // cider vinegar
Cut the tomatoes into different shapes (quarters, slices) and arrange them on a plate. Season with olive oil and vinegar, and then with the fleur de sel and a twist of pepper. Pour 2-3 tablespoons of elderberry syrup around the tomatoes and garnish with herbs and aromatic flowers.

Serves 8

'Ayurvedic' lobster from the Belgian coast
North Sea lobster on a bed of red lentil risotto with 'Ayurvedic' spices

Lobster bisque
2 lobsters as a starter (or 4 lobsters for a main dish) // 1 garlic clove // 2 onions // 2 carrots // 1 leek // 2 celery stalks // 1 large tablespoon tomato paste // 100 ml (3.4 fl oz) cognac // ½ tablespoon turmeric // 100 g (3.5 oz) of ginger // salt and five-spice powder// 1 teaspoon yuzu kosho

Sweat the finely chopped onion and garlic in butter. Add the lobster pieces and all the other ingredients except the yuzu kosho. Cover with water and season. Allow to simmer for about an hour, adding the yuzu kosho at the end. Remove the pieces of lobster and strain the bisque through a fine sieve.

Red lentil risotto with 'Ayurvedic' spices
200 g (7 oz) red lentils // 60 g (2.1 oz) peeled garlic // 60 g (2.1 oz) peeled ginger // 1 teaspoon turmeric // extra virgin olive oil // fleur de sel // lobster bisque // meat from the lobster claws

Take a deep pan and gently cook the finely chopped garlic in olive oil until golden brown. Add the lentils, the grated ginger, the turmeric and some salt. Stir for about 2 minutes, as for risotto, then pour in the lobster bisque to 1 cm above the lentils. Continue stirring for 7 minutes until the lentils are al dente. Finally, add the chopped meat from the lobster claws.

Blackberry juice
100 g (3.5 oz) blackberries or blackberry coulis // ¼ fresh espelette pepper or ½ cm (0.2 inch) dried bird's eye chilli // 40 g (1.4 oz) sugar // fleur de sel // a dash of olive oil // 1 tablespoon apple vinegar

Mix all the ingredients in a food processor and strain through a stainless steel tamis.

Spinach
200 g (7 oz) spinach, stalks removed// extra virgin olive oil // 1 pinch of fleur de sel

Heat a little olive oil in a pan and add the spinach leaves. Cook over high heat for 3 minutes until all the leaves are wilted. Season with a pinch of fleur de sel and some pepper.

Assembly
Place some spinach on a warm plate, followed by a spoonful of lentil risotto. Grill the lobster tail, cut into neat slices and arrange on top. Pour some hot bisque over the lobster and garnish with seasonal herbs. Arabelle chose Marigold, ice plant, beetroot and clover leaves.

Serves 8

Back to the roots

Wok of garden roots: salsify, burdock and yacón on a bed of einkorn wheat

Roots
200 g (7 oz) salsify // 300 g (10.6 oz) burdock // 200 g (7 oz) Jerusalem artichoke // 50 ml (1.7 fl oz) sesame oil // 25 g (0.9 oz) cane sugar // 40 ml (1.4 fl oz) mirin // 70 ml (2.4 fl oz) soy sauce // 70 ml (2.4 fl oz) sake // 190 g (6.7 oz) shiitake, cut into strips // 30 g (1 oz) kombu // 1 small dried bird's eye pepper // 40 g (1.40 oz) hemp seeds // 20 g (0.7 oz) sesame seeds // 50 g (1.8 oz) fresh seaweed // 15 g (0.5 oz) Goji berries

Wash the roots, and either peel or scrub clean. Cut them diagonally into slices of about 2-3 mm (0.08 – 0.12 inch). Soak the seaweed for 15 minutes, drain and add fresh water. Bring the water and seaweed to the boil, simmer for a few minutes and drain (this dashi can be used for soup). Cut the seaweed into fine strips of 2-3 mm (0.08 – 0.12 inch).

Cook the salsify and burdock in sesame oil in a wok until golden brown. Add the remaining ingredients and cook briefly over a high heat until the roots are al dente.

Einkorn
200 g (7 oz) einkorn wheat, soaked in water for 12 hours // 1 pinch fleur de sel // a dash of extra virgin olive oil
Cook the einkorn in boiling salted water for 4 minutes and drain. Mix with olive oil and fleur de sel.

Assembly
Put a tablespoon of einkorn into a deep dish and top with the root vegetables from the wok. Garnish with some slices of yacón, cut into flowers using a pastry cutter.

Vegan cheese platter

Basic vegan cheese
100 g (3.5 oz) plain cashew nuts // 20 g (0.7 oz) yeast // 1 tablespoon onion, finely chopped // ½ teaspoon garlic powder // 1 teaspoon salt // 400 ml (13.5 fl oz) soya milk // 17 g (0.6 oz) agar-agar // 5 tablespoons soya or coconut oil // 2 tablespoons clear miso // juice of half a lime // 1 teaspoon tomato concentrate // ½ teaspoon Espelette or cayenne pepper

The spices
1 teaspoon ground cumin // a pinch of pepper // 1 teaspoon black onion seeds

Mix the cashew nuts with the yeast, onions, garlic powder and salt in a food processor. Combine the soya milk, agar-agar, oil, miso, lemon juice and tomato concentrate in a saucepan and bring to the boil. Cook for 2 minutes. Add this to the food processor and mix everything together. To have a variety of cheeses, add a spice of your choice to each cheese. Pour the mixtures into round shapes and sprinkle each with some more of the chosen spice. The cheese will keep in the fridge for about a week.

Assembly
Arrange at least two different cheeses on the plate. Garnish to your own taste with flowers, seasonal greens, cherry tomatoes, blueberries, grape, kiwi ...

Serves around 18 portions

Fragrance of 3 fruits

Almond biscuit
400 ml (1.7 cup) egg whites // 300 g (10.5 oz) cane sugar // 400 g (14 oz) ground almonds // 120 g (4.2 oz) butter or olive oil

Whisk the egg whites until they are stiff. Add the sugar, ground almonds and melted butter. Pour the mixture into a 26 cm × 36 cm (10.2 inch × 14.1 inch) baking frame and bake for 20 minutes at 180 °C (356 °F). Allow to cool, then freeze.

Raspberry cream
1 l raspberry coulis // 8 whole eggs // 10 gelatine sheets

Mix together the coulis and eggs and cook at 80 °C (176 °F) until it coats the back of a spoon. Add the gelatine, previously soaked in cold water. Pour the coulis into the frame containing the biscuit base and return to the freezer.

Orange cream
1 l (1 quart) fresh orange juice // 10 whole eggs // 10 sheets of gelatine // 250 g (8.8 oz) icing sugar

Make the orange cream as above, including the icing sugar, pour into the frame and return it to the freezer.

Grapefruit cream
1 l (1 quart) grapefruit juice // 10 whole eggs // 10 sheets of gelatine // 250 g (8.8 oz) icing sugar

Make the grapefruit cream as above, pour it into the frame and return it to the freezer.

Four fruity gels
200 ml (6.8 fl oz) of 4 different juices: grapefruit, orange, lemon, raspberry (slightly diluted coulis) // 4 × 4 g (4 × 2.3 dr) agar-agar

Boil each juice separately for a minute with 4 g (2.3 dr) of agar-agar. Allow to cool. When thickened, lightly mix each gel and strain separately through a fine sieve. Put in four piping bags. Store in the fridge.

Sauce
200 ml (6.8 fl oz) raspberry coulis // 200 ml (6.8 fl oz) orange juice // 200 ml (6.8 fl oz) grapefruit juice // 200 ml (6.8 fl oz) orange flower water // 20 ml (0.7 fl oz) rose water // 25 g (0.9 oz) fresh mint // 25 g (0.9 oz) fresh coriander // 5 g (0.2 oz) black pepper // 250 g (8.8 oz) icing sugar

Mix all the ingredients together to capture the fragrance of the dessert as a whole. Blend in a food processor.

Pink rice leaf
100 g (3.5 oz) overcooked rice // 100 ml (3.4 fl oz) beetroot juice for natural colour // 1 tablespoon cane sugar

Blend all the ingredients in a food processor and spread the mixture on a silicone mat. Put in the oven to dry at 100 °C (212 °F) for 10-15 minutes.

Macaroon
90 g (3.2 oz) egg white // 60 g (2.1 oz) egg yolk // 250 g (1 ¼ cup) unrefined cane sugar // ½ vanilla pod // 250 g (2 ¼ cup) flour, sifted // caster sugar

Scrape the seeds from the vanilla pod. Whisk the eggs with the vanilla seeds and sugar until creamy. Gently fold in the sifted flour using a spatula. Use a piping bag with a size 6 nozzle to make small balls of about 1 cm (0.4 inch) diameter on a silicone mat. Immediately sprinkle with caster sugar and leave to dry for about 3 hours in the open air. Preheat the oven and bake for 8-9 min at 150 °C (300 °F).

Assembly
Arrange a piece of the fruit cake and some gel dots on the plate and decorate with pink rice leaves and other small decorations. Finish with a drizzle of sauce.

In her restaurant, Arabelle sprays the original perfume on a paper strip so that it can be compared with the fragrance of the dessert.

7 HEALTHY RECIPES FOR A BUSINESS LUNCH

Trade missions

Godfather and monument of Belgian haute cuisine

More than three decades ago, a talented young chef embarked on a great adventure in Bruges. He opened his own restaurant, De Karmeliet, which would become a true monument in the Belgian gastronomic landscape. In 1996, Geert Van Hecke became the first Flemish chef with three stars on his chef's hat. His restaurant held onto those stars for 20 years until very recently when he decided to close its doors to lead a more quiet life. Although not quite so quiet, because a few doors away he has opened the cosy **Zet'Joe** ('be seated' in local dialect). Small in scale without compromising on quality, it is no surprise to see it, too, climb the Michelin ladder. The affable Van Hecke is not a man of trends. His cuisine is the embodiment of taste and flavour, centred on top quality, preferably local, ingredients. He never commits his recipes to paper for his brigade. His cooking is based on confidence, instinct and, above all, a great deal of tasting. Therefore it is a great honour that Chef Van Hecke was willing to write down his version of the queen of Belgian classics, the legendary 'Bouchée à la Reine'! Traditionally served in a puff pastry case, overflowing with a rich sauce of chicken, meatballs and mushrooms, Chef Van Hecke proposes his pure contemporary version: **'Bouchée à la Reine' of the Twenty-first Century** in honour of Her Highness Queen Mathilde.

We would like to leave you with Van Hecke's favourite saying: 'Cooking is as simple as happiness'. Something to remember when you are grumbling in your kitchen! – **www.zetjoe.be**

Geert Van Hecke

Serves 4

Bouchée à la Reine of the 21st century

Capon with leeks, little meatballs and mushrooms

Rooster
1 young capon (coucou de Malines) of +/- 600 g (1.3 lbs) // 1 l (1 quart) vegetable broth // 250 g (8.8 oz) mushrooms // 250 g (8.8 oz) oyster mushrooms // 2 leeks // puff pastry // fresh rosemary // juice of 1 lemon // 100 g (3.5 oz) butter
Boil the capon for 20 minutes over low heat in a vegetable broth. Set aside for about ten minutes. Cut the thighs and remove the fillets and skin.
Cover the fillet with overlapping finely sliced mushrooms and coat with lemon juice and melted butter. Keep warm in the oven.
Bake the capon skin between 2 heavy oven plates for about 12 minutes at 180 °C (356 °F). Break into irregular pieces. Cook the legs in some butter and olive oil. Season with pepper, salt and rosemary. Cook the oyster mushrooms in the same way.
Cut the leeks into 3 to 4 cm (0.1 to 0.15 inch) strips and boil them in salted water.
Carefully roll out the puff pastry and set aside for 2 hours. Prick the pastry before putting it in a preheated oven at 150 °C (300 °F). When baked, cut into triangles.

Chicken meatballs
1 chicken fillet // 1 coffee spoon mushroom powder (dried mushrooms) // 1 egg white // 150 ml (5.1 fl oz) whipping cream // pepper, salt, nutmeg and cayenne pepper
Put the chicken and egg white in a blender. Add the cream with a spatula and season with salt, pepper, nutmeg, cayenne pepper and the mushroom powder. Then roll into small balls and poach in salted water at about 80 °C (180 °F) for about twenty minutes.

Beer sauce
1 bottle of Deus beer // 500 ml (17 fl oz) whipping cream // 2 shallots, chopped // 1 clove of garlic // espelette pepper // 200 ml (6.8 fl oz) chicken stock // fresh rosemary // 2 egg yolks // lemon juice
Bring the stock, 200 ml (6.8 fl oz) beer, shallot, garlic and rosemary to the boil and allow to reduce. Add the cream and subsequently pour through a fine sieve to obtain a smooth sauce. Make a sabayon with the egg yolks and 50 ml (1.7 fl oz) of beer, then add the sauce while gently stirring. Season with salt, espelette pepper and a drizzle of lemon juice.

Assembly
Arrange some leek pieces in parallel on the plate. Place the fillet, chicken leg, meatballs and mushrooms on top. Add some sauce. Garnish with the puff pastry triangles and chicken skin, some black truffle according to taste and a sprig of rosemary.

A 21st century Royal dish should be paired with a 21st century Royal beer. The obvious choice is **Reserve Royale** and not just because of its name, which is a tribute to the Belgian Monarchy. The champagne bottle in which it is packaged, contains an exquisite artisanal beer that was awarded the Gold Medal for 'Best Belgian Blonde beer' at the World Beer Awards. Its Belgian origins are evident in its aromatic profile, which accentuates its rich and creamy mouthfeel and an intense taste of floral hops perfectly blended with a subtle hint of yeast.
www.reserveroyale.com

A special ambassador: Her Majesty Queen Mathilde

.be our guest

A SPECIAL AMBASSADOR: HER MAJESTY QUEEN MATHILDE

The fact that Chef Van Hecke dedicates his 'Bouchée à la Reine of the 21st Century' to Queen Mathilde, has everything to do with his admiration for the grace and dignity with which she carries out her functions day in and day out.

In the Kingdom of Belgium, the King is the symbol of the unity of the country. In many of his duties as head of state, the Queen is literally and figuratively at his side. Together they go on visits to every corner of the country and they honour ceremonies and events with their presence. Not only do they lend their ear to the man on the street, they also open the palace doors to receive national and foreign dignitaries with appropriate decorum as well as various ordinary people whom they wish to honour and meet.

Abroad, their State, and other, visits enhance the image and interests of Belgium. But there's more. In addition to her activities with the King, the Queen is very active on social and societal issues that are dear to her. She regularly visits social organisations, sometimes also supported through her own Fund. In addition, the Queen works tirelessly both at home and abroad for many charities including Child Focus and Unicef. Our Queen has also been appointed by the Secretary-General of the UN as a special ambassador for the UN Sustainable Development Goals (SDGs). She is above all an advocate for equality between men and women, and better access to education and healthcare for the least fortunate.

Queen Mathilde does all this with impeccable grace and style. Like no other she knows how to put Belgium on the map. Like no other she knows how to touch the hearts of those who cross her path. As a matter of course, she respects the strict rules of protocol and etiquette when necessary. But, with her natural charm, she can just as easily put protocol aside when it stands in the way of deeper human contact. Her innate empathy ensures that our Queen takes on an exemplary role wherever she goes. Anyone who has ever had the honour and pleasure of meeting her can testify that she always puts her guests at ease. Although the many receptions and meetings she hosts are catered for down to the last detail, both gastronomically and visually, her true hospitality lies in the personal attention that Queen Mathilde gives to each of her guests and conversation partners.

That is why Queen Mathilde is, like no other, an ambassador for Belgian hospitality.

.be our guest

7 cosmopolitan dishes to share

Diamonds, a sparkling ambassador for Belgium

.be our guest

DIAMONDS, A SPARKLING AMBASSADOR FOR BELGIUM

Did you know that nearly every diamond in the world has travelled through Antwerp at least once, rough or polished? The Antwerp diamond sector has been the undeniable world leader when it comes to diamond trading for over 570 years! Diamonds are also the most important Belgian export outside the European Union. And all this happens in the Antwerp diamond district, barely one square kilometer, where more than 1500 diamond dealers practise their trade and ensure a competitive market in all corners of the world. They have more than 70 different nationalities and very diverse religious, cultural and ethnic backgrounds. In today's world, this successful mix is something to cherish.

These diverse facets of the diamond sector naturally express themselves in Antwerp's gastronomic environment. In the many Antwerp eateries and restaurants you will meet and taste a melting pot of cultures. From Belgian to Arabic, Turkish to African, (South-)American to Asian ... you name it. The largest groups are the Indian and Jewish cultures, each with its own special cuisine: the Jain and the Yiddish respectively.

The Jain community comes from the Gujarat region, the birthplace of Mahatma Gandhi. They have absolute respect for every form of life, therefore no animal products are used in the Jain kitchen – with milk being the only exception. To the extent that is possible, one also avoids damaging plants during harvesting. The Jains therefore do not eat crops that grow in the soil, such as carrots or onions. They also do not drink alcohol. In that, they already differ significantly from the culinary rules of the orthodox Jews. These are laid down in the 'Kashrut', a series of laws that determine which ingredients may be eaten and which may not. For instance, only meat from ruminants with split hooves is kosher or 'clean'. Seafood, mollusks and shellfish are considered unclean, and only certain birds such as chicken and duck are considered kosher. It is also important that meat and dairy products remain separate. Kosher cooking therefore in practice requires a double kitchen: two cookers, two sinks, two sets of cutlery, etc.

It is wonderful that all these convictions, preferences and customs coexist smoothly and have produced positive dynamics for centuries. That is why the Antwerp Diamond sector is a unique ambassador of Belgian hospitality.

Passionate about vegetables, Seppe Nobels resolutely opts for a green menu. His trendy restaurant **Graanmarkt 13** is one of the 25 Best Vegetable Restaurants of the World. One of the pioneers of the Urban Farming Movement, Chef Nobels collects crispy fresh vegetables and herbs from his rooftop garden in the centre of Antwerp, to serve them immediately on your plate! It is a kitchen of the essence offering original flavour combinations and attaching great importance to their ecological footprint. As North Sea Chef, he also resolutely opts for North Sea fish, predominantly the lesser known bycatch. He is a chef in high demand for all kinds of events at home as well as abroad. You therefore might find this Food Rebel at Tomorrowland as well as in the Embassy of Belgium in New Delhi, in preparation for a state banquet for the Royal Couple.
www.graanmarkt13.be

Vegetables and diamonds: wonders of nature with many facets

In this international spirit, Chef Nobels presents a cosmopolitan menu in honour of the Diamond sector, which puts his city on the map worldwide. He proposes seven dishes which he links to the **Embassies of Belgium in Copenhagen** (Denmark), **Tel Aviv** (Israel) and **Ottawa** (Canada).

Seppe Nobels

Copenhagen (DENMARK)

Starter: Starter of the purest carat

Antwerp, international port city, owes a substantial part of its success to the sea. So too does Copenhagen with its world famous little mermaid. Scandinavian gravad lax sprinkled with spiced gin from the carob tree seed, razor clams from the North Sea with seaweed and asparagus in green sauce with eel and scandinavian sorrel; it is definitely a starter of the purest carat.

Tel Aviv (ISRAEL)

Main dish: 'Mazel und Brucha'

'Mazel und Brucha' (happiness and blessing). Even today, this traditional Yiddish phrase is still used in the Antwerp Diamond District when closing a deal. It is the perfect title for this triple dish which you can share with your guests. Labneh, hummus, and Jerusalem artichoke, these are just a few examples of the many mezzes of Israeli cuisine. With some Belgian twists such as juniper, parsnip, Flanders poppy seed and Tierenteyn mustard from Ghent, they sparkle even more.

Ottawa (CANADA)

Dessert: Antwerp 'pain perdu' Canadian style

Particularly for Canada, the world's third largest producer of diamonds, Chef Nobels prepares a hipster version of 'pain perdu', also known in England as the poor knights of Windsor. With a drizzle of Elixir d'Anvers and a combination of Liege syrup and the famous Canadian maple syrup, he is about to create a new North Atlantic Alliance for the gourmets among us.

Serves 4

Starter of the purest carat // Copenhagen

Gravlax of fennel and Diva Dark Gin (with carob seeds),
razor clams of the North Sea, mayonnaise with Elixir d'Anvers,
salicornia, dill or fennel leaves, asparagus 'in 't groen' (with green sauce),
eel and a touch of Scandinavian sorrel

Gravlax of fennel
3 fennel bulbs // 1 lime // 1 tablespoons pink peppercorns // 12 juniper berries // 1 pinch of piment d'Espelette // 1 tablespoon red chilli // fleur de sel // 1 tablespoon sugar // 3 tablespoons Diva Dark Gin // 80 g (2.8 oz) tapioca // 2 tablespoons mustard seed // 50 g (1.8 oz) fresh seaweed // 1 tablespoon white wine vinegar // a bunch of young basil // 2 tablespoons olive oil

Slice the fennel thinly using a mandolin. Place in a deep plate and add the lime juice, pink peppercorns, juniper berries, piment d'Espelette, finely chopped chilli, fleur de sel, sugar and gin on top. Cover with cling film and allow to marinate in the fridge for at least 4 hours.

Put the mustard seeds in a herb infuser and tie the seaweed together. Bring the tapioca, mustard seeds and seaweed to a boil. Add salt and vinegar to boiling water and allow to boil for 5 minutes. Then pour through a fine sieve and allow to cool to room temperature.

Arrange the fennel on a plate and garnish with some cooked tapioca, seaweed and mustard seeds, young basil leaves and a drizzle of olive oil.

Razor clams of the North Sea with mayonnaise
a piece of ginger // 50 ml (1.7 fl oz) sweet soy sauce // 2 tablespoons mustard // 1 tablespoon hoisin sauce // 2 tablespoons rice vinegar // 1 lime // 4 egg yolks // 200 ml (6.8 fl oz) peanut oil // salt and ground pepper // 2 tablespoons Elixir d'Anvers liqueur or similar liqueur // 16 razor clams // ½ lemon // 2 tablespoons olive oil // 100 g (3.5 oz) salicornia // dill or fennel leaves

Chop the ginger into 2 mm (0.08 inch) pieces. Squeeze the lime and lemon separately and grate some lemon zest. Mix the ginger, soy sauce, Elixir d'Anvers, mustard, hoisin sauce, rice vinegar, lime juice and egg yolks in a blender and make mayonnaise by gradually adding the peanut oil. Season with salt and pepper.

Rinse the razor clams with cold water, then place them in boiling water for about 5 seconds, until they open. Remove the meat from the clams and cut into small pieces. Season with finely chopped shallot, lemon zest, lemon juice, olive oil, salt and pepper.

Rinse the salicornia. Fill the razor clams with pieces of clam meat, mayonnaise and salicornia. Garnish with dill or fennel leaves and lemon zest.

Asparagus 'in 't groen' (with green sauce)
1 bunch Malines asparagus // 200 ml (6.8 fl oz) vegetable stock // 1 bunch chervil // 1 bunch parsley // 1 bunch curly parsley // 1 lemon // pepper and salt // 200 g (7 oz) smoked eel fillets // 2 tablespoons capers // 1 small bunch of sorrel clover // 1 small bunch of sorrel // vegetable stock

Peel the asparagus with a vegetable peeler. Hold each asparagus by its head and peel from top to bottom. Break the stiff tip of the asparagus. Then steam for 5 minutes until tender. Arrange the asparagus on a large plate and braise with a Bunsen burner until golden and sprinkle with sea salt.

Blend the vegetable stock with the chervil and the two types of parsley. Cut the lemon into wedges and add the remaining lemon juice to the green sauce. Season with salt and pepper.

Cut the eel into equal parts and grill in the oven until lukewarm.

Pour some green sauce in the middle of a deep plate. Place the asparagus and the eel parts on top. Garnish with lemon wedges, capers, and both types of sorrel.

DIVA Dark Gin was designed for the new DIVA diamond museum in Antwerp. This spicy gin makes reference to one of the basic terms used in the diamond sector, 'carat', which determines the weight of a diamond. The seeds of the carob tree, which grows mainly around the Mediterranean Sea, weighs exactly 0.2 g (3 gr) each. Since ancient times, this seed has been used to carry out precise measurements to weigh diamonds. The word 'carat' comes from the Greek name for the seed 'keratonia'. Dark Diva has a soft floral nose with vegetal notes and aromas of vanilla and cereals.
www.divagin.com

Copenhagen

Serves 4

'Mazel und Brucha'

// Tel Aviv

'Labneh' with Flanders poppy seed,
Belgian hummus of parsnip and mustard,
'Jerusalem artichoke'

'Labneh' with Flanders poppy seed
6 tomatoes (yellow and red) // 250 ml (8.5 fl oz) full fat yogurt // 2 tablespoons za'atar // 100 ml (3.4 fl oz) olive oil, plus some extra to sprinkle // ½ garlic clove // 100 g (3.5 oz) puff pastry // sea salt // 2 tablespoons poppy seed // salt and ground black pepper

To make garlic oil, heat the olive oil in a pan at 70 °C (160 °F), add the garlic and season with salt and pepper. Allow to cool and cover with cling film so that it can infuse for about four hours.

Preheat the oven to 185 °C (365 °F). Place baking paper on a baking sheet, roll out the puff pastry and prick several times with a fork. Sprinkle some sea salt, Flanders poppy seed and olive oil on top. Cover with a second baking paper and a heavy baking tin so that the puff pastry doesn't rise. Bake it in the oven for 12 minutes and break into pieces.

Assembly
Cut the tomatoes into 4 equal parts and take out the seeds. Spread yogurt on a plate, arrange the tomato seeds and crisp puffs on it. Finish with za'atar, Flanders poppy seed, sea salt and ground pepper. Drizzle some garlic oil just before serving.

Hummus of parsnip
150 g (5.3 oz) dry chickpeas // 3 parsnips // 1 litre soya milk // salt and pepper // pinch of cumin // fleur de sel // 2 tbsp of tahini // 3 tbsp of Tierenteyn mustard

Soak the chickpeas overnight in water and drain. Peel the parsnips and cut into pieces. Cook the vegetables in soya milk until tender. Put the chickpeas and the parsnips in a blender and add cumin, tahini, mustard, freshly ground pepper and salt. Blend everything together. Add some of the cooked soya milk until you obtain a smooth hummus.

Black olives powder
200 g (7 oz) black olives // 2 tbsp breadcrumbs

Remove the stones from the olives and dry them either in the oven at 60 °C (140 °F) for 12 hours or on a radiator for 3 nights. Blend dried olives into powder. If too moist, add 2 tablespoons of breadcrumbs.

Assembly
Spread the hummus onto the plate, drizzle garlic oil and garnish with the black olive powder.

'Jerusalem artichoke'
14 large Jerusalem artichokes // olive oil // 2 garlic cloves // 2 juniper berries // 2 bay leaves // 4 sprigs of thyme // 2 cloves // 2 star anise // young sprigs of thyme // 4 tablespoons soya milk

Scrub the Jerusalem artichokes until they are clean and cut 13 of them lengthwise in two.

Finely slice one Jerusalem artichoke and fry golden brown at 180 °C (360 °F). Sprinkle some fine salt on the chips.

Pour a lot of oil in a large pan and place the artichoke halves with the flat side down. Crush the garlic and ground the juniper berries in a mortar. Then add garlic, juniper berries, bay leaves, thyme, cloves and star anise to the artichokes and allow to simmer on low heat. Turn the artichokes after 10 minutes and allow to simmer for another 15 minutes. Take 6 half artichokes from the pan and blend them in a food processor together with 4 tablespoons of soya milk until you obtain a smooth cream. Put the cream into a piping bag.

Assembly
Arrange 5 artichoke halves on a plate and pipe some swirls of artichoke cream in between. Garnish with parsnip chips and young sprigs of thyme.

7 COSMOPOLITAN DISHES TO SHARE

Tel Aviv

Serves 4

Antwerp 'pain perdu' Canadian style

// Ottawa

Lost bread with Elixir d'Anvers and maple syrup, granola, buttermilk ice cream

Buttermilk ice cream
500 ml (1 pint) buttermilk // 125 ml (4.2 fl oz) water // 125 g (4.4 oz) cane sugar // 50 g (1.8 oz) glucose powder // juice of ½ lemon
Heat the water and sugar to 90 °C (195 °F). Allow to cool to room temperature. Stir the mixture together with the other ingredients and turn into ice cream using an electric ice cream maker.

Granola
80 g (2.8 oz) beechnuts // 80 g (2.8 oz) chopped chestnut // 40 g (1.4 oz) golden raisins // 120 g (4.2 oz) oats // 1 to 2 tablespoons of honey
Mix the nuts, raisins and oats in a bowl. Whisk the honey with an equal amount of water and mix everything together. Spread on a baking sheet with butter paper. Allow to caramelize in the oven at 175 °C (350 °F) for 25 minutes. Stir 4 times while baking. Make sure everything is completely dry.

Pain perdu with maple syrup and elixir d'Anvers
4 eggs // 100 ml (3.4 fl oz) Elixir d'Anvers liqueur // 100 ml (3.4 fl oz) milk // 1 tablespoon self-rising flour // 2 tablespoons of apple and pear syrup (Sirop de Liège) // 2 tablespoons of maple syrup // 4 large slices of sourdough bread // 2 pears
Beat the eggs together with the Elixir d'Anvers, milk, flour and syrup. Dip the bread slices in the egg mixture until they have absorbed all liquid. Heat a pan, melt the butter and pan fry the bread slices until golden brown. Also sauté one pear cut in four. Slice the other pear into fine strips.

Assembly
200 g (7 oz) berries to taste // 60 g (2.1 oz) crumbled meringue // 1 lime
Arrange a slice of pain perdu bread on the plate. Sprinkle some granola and crumbled meringue on top and add a spoon of buttermilk ice-cream. Garnish with strips of pear, a part of baked pear, berries and lime zest. Drizzle maple syrup.

Elixir d'Anvers, a delicious and invigorating liqueur from grandmother's time, is attributed remarkable digestive properties. The recipe of the Antwerp pharmacist-doctor François-Xavier de Beukelaer dating from 1863, has been awarded countless international marks of recognition, even from Louis Pasteur himself! The liqueur is still traditionally prepared with plants and herbs from all over the world. The ideal finishing touch to spice up a cosmopolitan dish!
www.elixirdanvers.be

7 COSMOPOLITAN DISHES TO SHARE

Ottawa

.be our guest

---
7 desserts

SWEET AND SALTY

Paul Wittamer will tell you that he is better known in Japan than in Belgium, which is quite remarkable, given the name and fame that **Maison Wittamer** has garnered over more than a century and three successive generations. The country's most famous confectionary and its adjoining chocolate shop, on the Grand Sablon in Brussels, are an attraction for tourists and cake aficionados alike. Even the Belgian Royal family recognises the exceptional craftsmanship of Chef Wittamer.

Maison Wittamer is a Purveyor to the Court and is regularly called upon to create special cakes whenever the Royal family has something special to celebrate.

In spite of his success, Paul Wittamer continues to run his business in a very down-to-earth manner, with boundless enthusiasm, while dedicated to the unique heritage of his family business and the countless apprentices he has taken under his wing to learn his craft. – **www.wittamer.com**

Purveyor to the Court and icon of artisanal craftsmanship

Paul Wittamer, considered to be a living legend in the world of confectionary, is happy to share the secrets of some of his favourite recipes. These are classics into which he has poured his ('sweet')heart and soul.

Paul Wittamer

Royal chocolate cake
Wittamer's famous 'Samba' cake is hidden beneath the tricoloured sugar icing. This work of art won first prize in the prestigious 'Relais Desserts de l'Entremets au Chocolat' competition. What makes the Samba so special? Try it and see!

Tricolour of fruit jellies
This is the luxury version of a natural sweet, a treat to serve with coffee or tea, a special addition to your dessert or just a delicious snack.

The 'Misérable'
The Misérable is a traditional Belgian patisserie. Can you think of any other country where a cake would be given such surreal name? Nobody seems to know where the name came from. But we have a suspicion that it might be because the last bite leaves you overwhelmed by sadness ... until it's time to eat another Misérable!

A feast of mini tartlets
What could be more welcoming than presenting an array of little tarts in various flavours so as to delight each and everyone of your guests. And it is not that complicated at all. Chef Wittamer shares his basic recipes for delicious finger food tartlets and puffs, which can be garnished according to taste and the inspiration of the moment.

Serves 12

Royal chocolate cake

You can make this cake in a traditional round baking tin or a ball shaped mould (as pictured).

Prince biscuit
35 g (1.2 oz) cocoa powder // 55 g (½ cup) flour // 8 egg yolks // 60 g (2.1 oz) ground almonds // 60 g (2.1 oz) icing sugar // 55 g (1.9 oz) butter // 145 ml (4.9 fl oz) egg whites // 60 g (2.1 oz) granulated sugar

Sift the cocoa and flour together. Beat the egg yolks with the ground almonds and icing sugar until thick and creamy. Add the melted butter and stir. Allow to rest. Beat the egg whites with the granulated sugar until stiff.
With a spatula, fold half of the egg whites into the egg yolk mixture. Add the flour and cocoa, followed by the remaining egg whites.
Pipe the mixture on a baking sheet, using a piping bag with a size 8 nozzle, in a round shape one size smaller than the cake ring that will be used for the assembly. Repeat so that you have two biscuits.
Bake for about 5 minutes in a preheated oven at 240 °C (460 °F).

Milk chocolate mousse
450 ml (15.2 fl oz) cream // 250 g (8.8 oz) milk chocolate // 75 g (2.6 oz) egg yolks // 120 ml (4 fl oz) syrup, made with 50 ml (1.7 fl oz) water and 70 g (2.5 oz) granulated sugar
Lightly whip the cream. Set aside.
Melt the chocolate gently in a bain marie or very carefully in the microwave.
Boil the granulated sugar with the water to make a syrup. Beat the egg yolks and pour the syrup on top. Bring this mixture to the boil again while slowly stirring with a spatula. When it coats the back of a spoon, strain through a fine sieve and beat until it is very light and fluffy.
Make a ganache with ⅓ of the whipped cream and the melted chocolate. Fold this chocolate cream into the egg mixture and add the remaining whipped cream. Stir until you have a smooth cream.

Dark chocolate mousse
450 ml (15.2 oz) whipping cream // 240 g (8.5 oz) chocolate, 70% cocoa // 80 g (2.8 oz) egg yolk // 135 ml (4.6 fl oz) syrup, made with 55 ml (1.9 fl oz) water and 80 g (2.8 oz) granulated sugar
Prepare in the same way as the milk chocolate mousse above.

Chocolate jelly (to finish)
150 ml (5 fl oz) water // 300 g (1 ½ cup) granulated sugar // 300 g (10.6 oz) glucose // 200 ml 6.8 fl oz) sweetened condensed milk // 50 g (1.8 oz) cocoa powder // 200 g (7 oz) chocolate, 65% cocoa // 7 sheets gelatine
Heat the water, sugar, glucose and condensed milk. When it starts to boil, add the cocoa and stir well. Bring back to the boil, remove from heat and add the gelatine, previously soaked in cold water. Stir well.

Assembly
Take a cake ring of 22 cm (8.7 inch) in diameter and about 4 cm (1.6 inch) in height. Put one Prince biscuit on the bottom of the mould, then half fill the mould with milk chocolate mousse. Put another biscuit on top. Fill with dark chocolate mousse and smooth the top.
Put the cake in the fridge for 2 hours. Remove the cake ring and coat with the chocolate jelly preheated to 35 °C (95 °F) (check with a cooking thermometer). Allow the cake to rest for a few minutes so that the coating sets.

For a 38 × 38 cm (14.96 inch),
1 cm (0.39 inch) high, baking tray

Tricolour fruit jelly

1 l (1 quart) strawberry juice // 100 ml (3.4 fl oz) lemon juice // 1.325 kg (6 ²/₃ cup) granulated sugar// 30 g (1 oz) yellow pectin (E440) // 105 g (3.7 oz) granulated sugar // 350 g (12.3 oz) glucose // 7.5 g (115 gr) citric acid // 10 ml (0.34 fl oz) water

Mix the yellow pectin with the 105 g (3.7 oz) of sugar. Mix in the strawberry and lemon juices, and bring to the boil. Add the glucose and the 1.325 kg (6 ⅔ cup) of sugar. Using a sugar thermometer, heat to 118 °C (245 °F). Turn off the heat and put aside. Mix the citric acid with the water and add this mixture to the jelly. Pour into the baking tray and leave to set.

For different flavours and colours, use the same recipe with one kilogram of the juice and/or pulp of another fruit, adjusting the amount of sugar, if needed, according to the acidity of the fruit chosen and your own preference.

To finish
1 kg (2.2 lbs) of granulated sugar
Cut the jelly into 2 cm × 2 cm (0.8 × 0.8 inch) squares and roll through the granulated sugar.

Serves 15

The 'Misérable'

Biscuit
250 g (8.8 oz) egg whites // 50 g (1.8 oz) granulated sugar // 250 g (8.8 oz) ground almonds // 250 g (8.8 oz) icing sugar // 50 g (1.8 oz) flour

Beat the egg whites with the granulated sugar until stiff peaks form. Mix together the ground almonds, flour and icing sugar. Scatter this mixture over the egg whites and mix. Divide the mixture between two 20 × 30 cm (7.9 × 11.8 inch) baking sheets, lined with greaseproof paper. The biscuit should be about 1.5 cm (0.6 inch) thick. Bake at 190 °C (375 °F) for about 30 to 40 minutes.

Cream 'Misérable'
250 ml (1 cup) water // 260 g (9.2 oz) sugar // 1 vanilla pod // 8 egg yolks // 625 g (1.4 lbs) room temperature butter

Bring the water to the boil, add the vanilla pod and turn off the heat. Allow to rest for 5 minutes, then strain through a fine sieve. Put in a saucepan along with the sugar and boil until you have a syrup. While still boiling hot, pour half the syrup over the egg yolks and whisk. Then pour this mixture into a saucepan and cook over low heat, taking care not to let it boil. Continue stirring until the cream coats the back of a spoon. Remove from the heat and pour everything into a food processor. Process gently until the cream cools down. When the mixture is almost cold, gradually whisk in the butter. Store in the fridge.

Assembly
Put one biscuit cooked side down. Pour the cream over the biscuit and spread it out to the edges. Top with another biscuit cooked side up, lightly press and put in the fridge for 2 hours.

To finish
Remove from the fridge, pour some icing sugar on top and spread well with your fingers so that any crevices in the biscuit are filled. Using a sieve, sprinkle more icing sugar on top until you have a smooth surface.

A feast of mini tartlets

Pastry cream (750 g)
500 g (16.7 oz) milk // ½ vanilla pod // 6 egg yolks // 40 g (1.4 oz) cornflour // 125 g (²/₃ cup) granulated sugar
Cut the vanilla pod lengthwise. Boil half the pod with the milk. In a bowl, whisk the egg yolks and sugar until thick and creamy, then add the cornflour. Pour the egg mixture over the hot milk, whisking lightly, and bring to the boil. Boil for one minute, whisking vigorously. Then pour the cream into a bowl, covering the surface with clingfilm to prevent a skin forming.

Mini eclairs (1.5 kg (3.3 lbs))
250 ml (8.5 fl oz) milk // 250 ml (8.5 fl oz) water // 225 g (7.9 oz) butter // 5 g (2.8 dr) salt // 10 g (5.6 dr) caster sugar // 270 g (9.5 oz) flour // 10 eggs
Bring the water, milk, sugar, salt and butter to the boil. When it reaches boiling point, add the flour and stir vigorously with a wooden spoon until the mixture is smooth and no longer sticks to the sides. Allow to cook for 2 minutes. Put the dough in a food processor and mix until it cools to room temperature. Then gradually add the whole eggs while mixing at medium speed until you have a smooth dough. The dough can very easily be frozen, raw or cooked, without affecting it.

To make mini eclairs, fit a piping bag with a 1.5 cm (0.6 inch) round nozzle. Pipe 6 cm (2.4 inch) lengths onto a greased baking sheet. Press down any peaks with a wetted finger. Bake in an oven preheated to 220 °C (430 °F) and bake until firm and lightly golden. Do not open the oven during baking as the eclairs could collapse. Remove the eclairs from the oven, slice lengthwise, then put the halves again in the oven for a few minutes to dry and get crispy. When cold, fill with piped pastry cream. Dip in melted chocolate or coffee icing and allow to set.

Mini tartlets (1.2 kg (2.6 lbs))
500 g (4 1/5 cup) flour // 300 g (1 ¼ cup) butter // 180 g (6.3 oz) granulated sugar // a pinch of salt // 2 eggs // 60 g (2.1 oz) ground almonds // 60 g (2.1 oz) icing sugar
Soften the butter before adding the sugar, almonds and a pinch of salt. Knead until smooth. Add the eggs, and then the flour. When smooth, wrap the dough in clingfilm and leave to rest in the fridge for 2 hours.
Roll out the pastry and cut out rounds with a cookie cutter. Press into mini tartlet shells. Bake at 200 °C (390 °F) until golden brown. Fill with whipped or pastry cream, and garnish with seasonal fruit, according to taste.

Chocolate, Belgium's most excellent ambassador

.be our guest

CHOCOLATE, BELGIUM'S MOST EXCELLENT AMBASSADOR

Nowhere in the world are people as besotted with chocolate as in Belgium. In any year the average Belgian indulges in 6 kilos of it. For a Belgian, chocolate is a way of life – wherever he finds himself he'll visit the local chocolate museum, he'll gladly take part in any outing which involves chocolate, he signs up for tastings with the most innovative chocolate makers and he lets nothing get between him and a workshop on the latest trends in the world of chocolate.

As a tourist, it's impossible to avoid being caught up in this passion. At every turn there are beautiful chocolate shops overflowing with pralines, chocolate fountains, lollipops, and chocolate bars in every size and colour ... Even your cup of coffee is served with a praline! And chances are that the local bakery also sells their own hand-crafted chocolate creations. A city break in Belgium is fraught with danger for those on a diet ...

So, how did it come to this? The first seeds of this chocolate mania were planted in the middle of the 19th century. The Brussels pharmacist, *Jean Neuhaus*, decided to mask the unpleasant taste of his medicines by coating them in a layer of chocolate. His grandson took hold of this clever idea and in 1912 he encased delicious fillings in the chocolates. And so the first praline was born and a success story began. Even more so a few years later, when his enterprising wife designed the ballotin, the elegant praline box. Ever since chocolate has becomes a luxury gift and chocolate marketing has taken off. And more Belgian innovations followed. For example, *Charles Callebaut* found a market for his liquid couverture chocolate, *Basile Kestekidès*, nephew of the founder of Leonidas, launched the 'Manon', the famous white praline filled with a hazelnut embedded in buttercream. Then it was *Jacques'* turn to launch praline-filled chocolate bars and *Cote d'Or* invented the chocolate spread ... And the list goes on and on, with most recently the invention of 'pink chocolate'!

Currently, there are more than 320 Belgian chocolatiers (*Neuhaus, Godiva, Marcolini, Mary, Del Rey, The Chocolate Line by Dominique Persoone, Belcolade, Leonidas, Daskalides, Corné Port Royal, Guylian, Café-Tasse, Galler, Newtree, Dolfin, Starbrook Airlines, Belvas, Chocolat Essentiel, Chocolaterie Delvaux, Renardy, Laurent Gerbaud, Benoit Nihant, Zaabär, Van Dender, Chocolatier Dumon, Debailleul, Wittamer, Darcis, Chocolatier M,* etc ...), some more famous than others, each with their own specialties and flavour combinations. The success of Belgian chocolate can be attributed to the creativity and entrepreneurship of each one of them. And, of course, to the quality of the chocolate, for which Belgium is famous. After all, the largest chocolate factory in the world is located in Wieze, Belgium. *Barry Callebaut*, which is the world's most important supplier of industrial chocolate, produces around 270,000 tons of chocolate every year, and exports it to every corner of the world.

Simply because of the pleasure chocolate elicits around the globe and because a box of Belgian pralines always tastes better when shared, chocolate is an excellent ambassador for Belgian hospitality.

But do not forget: 'Life is like a box of chocolates – you never know what you're going to get ...'

Chocolatier M is the brand name of David Maenhout's chocolate line which he developed in his home town of Knokke, a mundane coastal resort. Maenhout has emerged as a trendsetter in the land of chocolate, not just in Belgium. The world press spotted this magician of taste sensations at the launch of his umami praline, in which he manages to sublimate this fifth basic taste into a surprising chocolate creation. A real world first! Since then, the recognition and awards both at home and abroad have been piling up. In Belgium, his praline based on sea buckthorn, freshly picked at the coast, has been recognized as a regional product. Chef Maenhout was the first to be proclaimed 'Chocolatier of the Year'. Internationally, two other gems from his chocolate range have recently been proclaimed best praline in the world: the dark chocolate 'Gin Tonic' and the milk chocolate 'Orient'. Top quality pralines fusing surprising flavour combinations and textures, are the trademark of this passionate chocolate designer who is all the rage wherever he is tasted.
www.chocolatier-m.be

Chef Maenhout, the official Belgian Chocolate Ambassador, is the right person to excite you with some fun chocolate recipes. He has gladly made them in honour of the **Embassy of Belgium in Abidjan**, Ivory Coast, the largest exporter of cocoa beans in the world.

David Maenhout

World class with his trendy fusion pralines

Chocolate lollipops
Nice to serve with coffee, to garnish a dessert, brighten up a reception or just to keep the children happy at home.

Cold minty chocolate drink
Refreshing on hot spring and summer days.

Belgian brownie
You can enjoy this chocolate cake at any time – in summer topped with lightly whipped vanilla-flavoured cream and fresh raspberries, or in winter, served on a nut and raisin crumble, briefly soaked in rum and then flambéed …

For about 50 lollipops

Chocolate lollipops

500 g (1.1 lbs) Callebaut dark chocolate 70%, preferably single origin or single-plantation // long wooden skewers
According to your own creativity:
Flavouring: candied fruit powder, cinnamon, curry powder …
Decoration: fleur de sel, pink peppercorns, roasted sesame seeds, small pieces of plain or caramelised nuts, mixed nuts and raisins, candied fruit, mint leaves, freeze-dried berry powder, crumbled babelutte or other hard candy, rose petals …

Arrange the sticks on baking paper or clingfilm that has been sprinkled with your favourite flavouring.
Melt 440 g (1 lb) of the chocolate at a low setting in the microwave. Stir regularly to prevent the chocolate from burning. Add the remaining 60 g (2.1 oz) of chocolate, which has been chilled in the fridge for at least an hour. Stir until all the pieces have melted and the chocolate is smooth.
Put the chocolate into a plastic piping bag, cut off a fine point at the tip and fix the stick with a large drop of chocolate. Then pipe the desired shapes, for example, different circles one over the other. Always make sure that the circles and the chocolate drop are connected.
Decorate immediately, allowing your imagination to run wild and using the garnishes of your choice, in any combination. The possibilities are endless. It's up to you!

Allow the lollipops to set in a cool place. Remove very carefully from the film and arrange them, standing upright, in a deep bowl filled, for example, with cocoa nibs, pink peppercorns or sesame seeds. You can also stick the lollipops into a large piece of exotic fruit, ice cream or cake.

Serves 4 to 6

Cold minty chocolate drink

85 g (3 oz) dark Callebaut chocolate, 70% cocoa // 85 ml (2.9 fl oz) cream // 15-20 g (0.5 – 0.7 oz) mint leaves from the garden // 16 g (9 dr) cane sugar // 135 g (4.8 oz) mineral water // optional: 10 ml (0.3 fl oz) dark rum

Bring the cream and the mint leaves to the boil. Cover with a lid to create a natural vacuum and allow to infuse for at least 15 minutes. Add the sugar and briefly return to the boil. Strain the cream through a sieve onto the chocolate pieces and stir continuously until you have a smooth even mixture. Then gradually add the water while stirring. Put in the fridge to cool.

If you like a mouthwarming feel, add some rum just before serving it ice cold in cocktail glasses. Top with fresh mint leaves and enjoy!

You can create a number of variations on this drink, using lavender flowers (sparingly to avoid them overwhelming the taste) or lemon balm leaves instead of the mint leaves.

Serves 6 to 8

Belgian brownie with nuts and candied fruit

360 g (12.7 oz) dark Callebaut chocolate, 70% cocoa, preferably single origin with fruity notes // 250 g (1 cup) butter // 3 eggs // 260 g (9.2 oz) dark brown sugar // 80 g (²/₃ cup) flour // 5 g (77 gr) baking powder // pinch of fleur de sel // pinch of cinnamon // vanilla extract // 50 g (1.8 oz) chopped roasted hazelnuts // 50 g (1.8 oz) chopped walnuts // 20 g (0.7 oz) chopped pistachio nuts // 50 g (1.8 oz) candied lemon or bergamot // some pieces of candied ginger

Gently melt the chocolate with the butter in a bain marie or in the microwave, and stir until smooth. Add the nuts, candied fruit, cinnamon and a few drops of vanilla extract. In another bowl mix the eggs with the sugar, and fold into the chocolate mixture. Mix the sifted flour with the baking powder and salt, and add to the chocolate mixture. Grease a 25 cm (9.8 inch) round baking tin, dust with flour and fill with the mixture. Bake for about 40 minutes in a preheated oven at 170 °C (340 °F) to 175 °C (350 °F). Allow the brownie to cool for about 35 minutes before removing from the tin.

Abidjan

Belgium may be renowned for its many tasty beers and excellent chocolate, but did you know that there are also more than 300 Belgian cheeses offering superb flavours of international quality? What's more, the Belgian **Nathalie Vanhaver** has joined the world of top cheese masters by winning gold at the 'Concours Mondial du Meilleur Fromager' in France. Nathalie thus became the first European woman to hold this title. Together with her husband Luc Callebaut, she runs a cheese specialty shop in Oudenaarde. By proposing this stunning little cheese platter, she has expressed her passion for her profession. It is a fascinating discovery of 7 special artisan cheeses, all prepared with fresh, raw milk.
www.kaasmeester-callebaut.be

Nathalie Vanhaver

A passionate cheese master of world class

How to compose a cheese platter?

For an interesting taste experience you ideally combine fresh, soft, semi-hard, blue-veined and hard cheeses, building up from soft to strong in taste. You should also take into account the different cheese families: from goat, sheep, white mold, cream cheese, semi-hard, to washed, hard and blue. Just a small bite or a main dish? Count about 250 g (8.8 oz) per person for a meal and feel free to choose from 7 to 8 cheese families. If you make a dessert platter, then 100-150 g (3.5 – 5.3 oz) per person is more than sufficient, depending on whether, in addition, sweets will be served afterwards. Maximum 5 pieces of cheese will do.

How to store cheese?

Cheese is a living product whose taste evolves. Temperature plays a major role. Cheeses should therefore be stored in the fridge or in the cellar. Make sure to cover the cheeses, otherwise they will dry or absorb flavours from other products. Also, do not place different cheese families under one dome. In order to render their full flavour, bring the cheeses to room temperature by taking them out half an hour to an hour before serving.

How to present a cheese platter?

Cheeses are available in all shapes and colours. By combining cheeses cut in different forms, you can make an interesting linear pattern. Round and square cheeses should be halved first, then cut in wedges (like a pie). Cylindrical cheeses are cut into slices and then in halves or triangles, according to taste. Flat, long cheeses are cut into triangles. Semi-hard and hard rectangular cheeses should be served in slices, cubes or sticks. Provide a separate knife for each cheese. This way you prevent flavours mingling

Sweet, salty and savoury garnish

Bread is fundamental when you serve cheese, because it neutralises and balances the strongest flavours. For example, crispy white bread to spread a ripe creamy cheese, nut bread for a soft blue cheese and a thick slice of farmer's bread for abbey cheese. Raisin bread is very tasty with more salty blue cheese or a firm old cheese. Nathalie serves refined Bruges rusks with her cheese platter.

Nuts, grapes and raisins? Of course, but there is more. Fruit provides some fresh notes on the cheese platter as well as in the mouth. For example, fresh figs or an aromatic pear go perfectly well with blue cheese. The following are also nice and fresh: apple pieces, fresh tomatoes, radish, watercress, celery or cucumber. Also honey, mustard, pickles, gherkin and silver onions make a cheese dish swing and hard old cheeses love, for example, all kinds of chutneys. But also jams can also do the trick. Don't hesitate to experiment!

What drink to serve with cheese?

Why not a nice Belgian beer? Soft, creamy cheeses go well with light beers (lager, white beer, fruity and spicy beers). The lighter the cheese, the lighter the beer. To accompany cheeses with a strong flavour, go for the Trappist (double or triple), abbey beer or other specialty beers. White wine also goes particularly well with cheese. If you are a red wine lover, avoid too many tannins, because they weigh heavily on the taste experience of the cheese. And finally, don't forget tea, either green or black, which harmoniously complement a cheese tasting.

BELGIAN CHEESE PLATTER

Clockwise (p. 221), Nathalie has selected the following highlights, which gradually become more and more specific in taste:

1. **Buche Cendrée** from the province of Namur, close to the Belgian Ardennes. Every year, the 'Route du Fromage' takes place in that region. It is a discovery walk where people meet cheese artisans and producers of regional products. This product from the Fromagerie du Gros-Chêne, is a **cylindrical goat's cheese** covered by an ash layer. It is a fresh starter with a slightly acidic touch.
www.groschene.be

2. **T'Zandmanneke** from the Westhoek, West Flanders. It is a soft, creamy, **surface-ripened cow's milk cheese** with a velvety taste, somewhere in between brie and camembert. It really melts on the tongue. You can definitely taste the passion of De Beauvoordse Walhoeve, a farmer's family with a natural view on food.
www.beauvoordse-walhoeve.be

3. **Brebis de Brakel** from the Flemish Ardennes, East-Flanders. On the farm 'De Schapenmelkerij' fresh milk from Belgian Milk Sheep is processed into young (8 to 10 weeks) **solid sheep cheese**. Brebis de Brakel has a mild and accessible taste with a delicious sweet touch, which evolves into beautiful nutty tones after 8 months of aging.
www.schapenkaas.be

4. **Tomme de Saint Servais** from Werbomont, province of Liège. The cheese plant Fromagerie des Ardennes produces this butter-fresh organic **hard cheese** with a beautiful, natural washed crust. The cheese has won several prizes. After a ripening process of at least two months, the taste of the rich cow's milk can be fully appreciated.
www.bioferme.be

5. *Pavé de Soignies* from Soignies, province of Hainaut. This square **cow's milk cheese** has a fresh, **sharp taste** – similar to a Pont-l'Evêque – with hints of heather flowers. It is a resilient, rather soft cheese with a washed edible crust. It is made with love in the Ferme le Bailly from the milk of some 180 home-grown cows, most of whom are called by their name.
www.lebailli.be

6. **Herve BOB** from Herve, Province of Liège. Undoubtedly one of the most **outstanding cheeses** of our country, a real treat. The Fromagerie du Vieux Moulin is the only cheese factory using **raw cow's milk** to produce Herve. This results in a creamy structure with salty notes. Together with Ardennes butter, Herve cheese is the only Belgian product with the Protected Designation of Origin (PDO) label. Beginners better start with the mild version, matured for only three weeks. Subsequently, you can proceed to the spicy Herve which has matured for 5 to 6 weeks and has powerful aromas typical of a washed crust cheese.
www.fromagerie-du-vieux-moulin.be

7. **Grevenbroecker** from Hamont-Achel, Province of Limburg. Catharinadal dairy farm produces this sophisticated **blue cheese** with a unique 'marble' blue-veined design, obtained by carefully stacking curds. Partly because of the relatively low salt levels, the result is rather creamy and refined yet with some spiciness. Served with cacao nibs, orange marmalade, fine dark Belgian chocolate with sea salt and lemon thyme, this is definitely the bouquet final of our cheese platter.
www.catharinadal.be

BELGIAN HOSPITALITY ON THE WEB

Diplomacy and foreign trade
Federal
abh-ace.be
autrementphenomenale.be
belgium.be
diplomatie.belgium.be
focusonbelgium.be

Regional
awex-export.be
flandersinvestmentandtrade.com
hub.brussels
investinbrussels.com

Belgian chefs and gastronomy
connaitrelawallonie.wallonie.be/fr/gastronomie
flandersfoodfaculty.be
gastronomie-wallonne.be
generationw.be
mastercooks.be
northseachefs.be
visitflanders.com: flanders-kitchen-rebels

Beer
belgium.beertourism.com
belgianbrewers.be
belgianfamilybrewers.be
belgiansmaak.com

Belgian Fries
belgapom.be
jamesbint.be
navefri-unafri.be

Cheese
bcz-cbl.be

Chocolate
choprabisco.be

Wine and spirits
belgianwines.com
odeflander.be
vigneronsdewallonie.be
vinumetspiritus.be

Food
apaqw.be
bedelicious.be
biendecheznous.be
fevia.be
food.be
freshfrombelgium.com

Tourism
Brussels: visitbrussels.be
Flanders: visitflanders.com; toerismevlaanderen.be
Wallonia: walloniabelgiumtourism.co.uk
German speaking community: ostbelgien.eu

By Province: visithainaut.be; luxembourg-belge.be; paysdesvallees.be; provincedeliege.be; destinationbw.be; toerismevlaamsbrabant.be; toerismelimburg.be; tov.be; westtoer.be; provincieantwerpen.be

brusselsairlines.com

THANK YOU TO

Our Ambassadors of Belgian hospitality: the top chefs, barman, beer sommelier, chocolatier, cheese master and pâtissier, who have gracefully shared their expertise and time.

The Federal Public Service Foreign Affairs, Foreign Trade and Development Cooperation – the offices of Press and Communication, Economic interests and Protocol – and in particular Ambassador Didier Vanderhasselt for their support. Also a big thank you to the Ambassadors Francoise Gustin, Rudy Veestraeten and Gerard Cockx, as well as Yves De Backer, Thibaut de Kerchove, Caroline Piret, Karel Tousseyn, Lisa Raes and Elke Van den Bosch.

The Embassies and Consulates-General of Belgium in Abidjan, Abu Dhabi, Amman, Bangkok, Berlin, Budapest, Canberra, Chennai, The Hague, Guangzhou, Istanbul, Copenhagen, London, Madrid, Moscow, New Delhi, Ottawa, Paris, Beijing, Pretoria, Rio de Janeiro, Rome, Tel Aviv, Tokyo, Tunis, Washington and Vienna. In particular, we could count on the support of **Ambassadors** Marie-France André, Olivier Belle, Marc Calcoen, Frank Carruet, Hugues Chantry, Hubert Cooreman, Raoul Delcorde, Ghislain d'Hoop, Chris Hoornaert, Rudy Huygelen, Philippe Kridelka, Jan Luykx, Vincent Mertens de Wilmars, Dominique Mineur, Marc Mullie, Leo Peeters, Jean-Arthur Régibeau, Gunther Sleeuwagen, Michel-Etienne Tilemans, Hendrik Van de Velde, Willem van de Voorde, Marc Vinck, Dirk Wouters and **Consuls-General** Jean-Paul Charlier, Sophie De Smedt, Joris Salden, Mark Van de Vreken, and **their spouses, partners or family members** who opened their doors with much enthusiasm, in particular Miek Calcoen-Declercq, Catharine d'Hoop, Hoda El Maghraby, Hilde Hermans, Marianne Huygelen-Lesceu, Fabio Melchiorri, Kathleen Missotten, Rachel Mubake, Marjolijn Mullie-van de Geer, Raka Singh-Luykx, Catherine Tilemans, Annekatrien Vinck, Katrin Wouters-Van Bragt as well as the **Embassy staff** Yildiz Asan, Olga Cogen, Sophie Damme, Gwenda De Moor, José de Pierpont, Daan Geysen, Dominique Freches, Yvan Gnaman, Nicole Opsommer, Siriporn Ouransathien, Andrzey Pyrka, Evie Ruymbeke, Philippe Sequaris, Anita Simon, Tristan Terryn, Mevr. Theuerkauff, Philippe Vagenhende, Simone Van den Bosch, Megan van der Westhuizen, Floretta Vanelslander.

Chefs and sommeliers linked to certain embassies: Christian Caluwaerts (Marriott Bangkok), M. Channa, Fabrice Leblus (Puratos/Gallothai), Dries Molkens, Christoph Pouls, Mme. Mew, Karl, Nooror and Sandra Steppé (Blue Elephant) and their team, M. Thong.

Photographer Heikki Verdurme, with an infallible intuition for aesthetics.

The English language wizzards and friends: Paula Fitzmaurice-Hanney for her precision and enthusiasm and Shashi Droesse for being available.

De Belgian tableware companies Eternum, PTZE Porselein, Val Saint Lambert and Verilin for the beautiful table in the Egmont Palace.

Last but not least, **our fantastic families**: Willem, Alexander, Bruno, Elinor and Sibylla van de Voorde and Johan, Kasper, Marnix, Vincent and Quinten Verkammen.

Egmont Palace, Tapestry Room – Reception Area for Foreign Guests

www.lannoo.com
Register on our web site and we will regularly send you a newsletter with information about new books and interesting, exclusive offers.

Text: **Kathleen Billen and Kristin van de Voorde-Heidbüchel**

English review: **Paula Fitzmaurice-Hanney**

Recipes: **Maxime Collard, Gert De Mangeleer, Bart De Pooter, Sang Hoon Degeimbre, Dimitry Lysens and Aagje Moens, David Maenhout, Yves Mattagne, Arabelle Meirlaen, Seppe Nobels, Pierre Résimont, Lionel and Laurence Rigolet, Geert Van Hecke, Jan Vandenplas, Albert Verdeyen and Marc Van Staen, Paul Wittamer**

Photography: **Heikki Verdurme**

Other images:
Fabrice Debatty (p. 36), Jan Crab (p. 88, 89), Harald Klemm (p. 110 above, p. 158 above)
Agnes Matthysen-Aerts (p. 175 and backcover), Donald Woodrow and Ilan Taché (p. 184), Xavier Harcq (p. 202).
The embassy photos were provided by the embassies themselves.

Graphic design: **Leen Depooter – quod. voor de vorm.**

If you have observations or questions, please contact our editorial office:
redactielifestyle@lannoo.com

© Lannoo Publishers, Tielt, 2018
D/2018/45/446 – NUR 440
ISBN 978 94 014 4982 3

Be our guest also exists in French (ISBN 978 94 014 4980 9) and Dutch (ISBN 978 94 014 4979 3)

All rights reserved. Nothing from this publication may be copied, stored in an automated database and/or be made public in any form or in any way, either electronic, mechanical or in any other manner without the prior written consent of the publisher.

Gastvrijheid – Hospitalité – Hospitality – Gastfreundschaft – Hospitalidade – Hospitalidad – 好客 – 好客 – Misafirperve
– การต้อนรับ – مرك الضيافة – Terranga – Gasvryheid – Ho Amohela Baeti – Kuamukela Tivakashi – Kamogelo ya Ba
Hospitalidade – Hospitalidad – 好客 – 好客 – Misafirperverlik – おもてなし – Гостеприимство – Akwaba
Amohela Baeti – Kuamukela Tivakashi – Kamogelo ya Baeng – Kugamuchira Vaeni – Gæstfrihed – Satkaar – सत्कार –
おもてなし – Гостеприимство – Akwaba – Vendégszerete – Ospitalità – Hahnassat orhim – חרוא תסנכה
Kugamuchira Vaeni – Gæstfrihed – Satkaar – सत्कार – Gastvrijheid – Hospitalité – Hospitality – Gastfreundschaft –
Vendégszerete – Ospitalità – Hahnassat orhim – מיחרוא תסנכה – การต้อนรับ – مرك الضيافة – Terranga – Gasvryheid
Gastvrijheid – Hospitalité – Hospitality – Gastfreundschaft – Hospitalidade – Hospitalidad – 好客 – 好客 – Misafirperve
– การต้อนรับ – مرك الضيافة – Terranga – Gasvryheid – Ho Amohela Baeti – Kuamukela Tivakashi – Kamogelo ya Bae
Hospitalidade – Hospitalidad – 好客 – 好客 – Misafirperverlik – おもてなし – Гостеприимство – Akwaba
Amohela Baeti – Kuamukela Tivakashi – Kamogelo ya Baeng – Kugamuchira Vaeni – Gæstfrihed – Satkaar – सत्कार –
おもてなし – Гостеприимство – Akwaba – Vendégszerete – Ospitalità – Hahnassat orhim – חרוא תסנכה
Kugamuchira Vaeni – Gæstfrihed – Satkaar – सत्कार – Gastvrijheid – Hospitalité – Hospitality – Gastfreundschaft –
Vendégszerete – Ospitalità – Hahnassat orhim – מיחרוא תסנכה – การต้อนรับ – مرك الضيافة – Terranga – Gasvryheid
Gastvrijheid – Hospitalité – Hospitality – Gastfreundschaft – Hospitalidade – Hospitalidad – 好客 – 好客 – Misafirperver
– การต้อนรับ – مرك الضيافة – Terranga – Gasvryheid – Ho Amohela Baeti – Kuamukela Tivakashi – Kamogelo ya Bae
Hospitalidade – Hospitalidad – 好客 – 好客 – Misafirperverlik – おもてなし – Гостеприимство – Akwaba
Amohela Baeti – Kuamukela Tivakashi – Kamogelo ya Baeng – Kugamuchira Vaeni – Gæstfrihed – Satkaar – सत्कार –
おもてなし – Гостеприимство – Akwaba – Vendégszerete – Ospitalità – Hahnassat orhim – חרוא תסנכה
Kugamuchira Vaeni – Gæstfrihed – Satkaar – सत्कार – Gastvrijheid – Hospitalité – Hospitality – Gastfreundschaft –
Vendégszerete – Ospitalità – Hahnassat orhim – מיחרוא תסנכה – การต้อนรับ – مرك الضيافة – Terranga – Gasvryheid
Gastvrijheid – Hospitalité – Hospitality – Gastfreundschaft – Hospitalidade – Hospitalidad – 好客 – 好客 – Misafirperve
– การต้อนรับ – مرك الضيافة – Terranga – Gasvryheid – Ho Amohela Baeti – Kuamukela Tivakashi – Kamogelo ya Bae
Hospitalidade – Hospitalidad – 好客 – 好客 – Misafirperverlik – おもてなし – Гостеприимство – Akwaba
Amohela Baeti – Kuamukela Tivakashi – Kamogelo ya Baeng – Kugamuchira Vaeni – Gæstfrihed – Satkaar – सत्कार –
おもてなし – Гостеприимство – Akwaba – Vendégszerete – Ospitalità – Hahnassat orhim – חרוא תסנכה
Kugamuchira Vaeni – Gæstfrihed – Satkaar – सत्कार – Gastvrijheid – Hospitalité – Hospitality – Gastfreundschaft –
Vendégszerete – Ospitalità – Hahnassat orhim – מיחרוא תסנכה – การต้อนรับ – مرك الضيافة – Terranga – Gasvryheid
Gastvrijheid – Hospitalité – Hospitality – Gastfreundschaft – Hospitalidade – Hospitalidad – 好客 – 好客 – Misafirperve
– การต้อนรับ – مرك الضيافة – Terranga – Gasvryheid – Ho Amohela Baeti – Kuamukela Tivakashi – Kamogelo ya Bae
Hospitalidade – Hospitalidad – 好客 – 好客 – Misafirperverlik – おもてなし – Гостеприимство – Akwaba